Here till the End

The Case for the Post-tribulation Rapture Position:
Exposing the Pre-tribulation Rapture Position

SCOTT A. WHEELER, RT (R) (MR) (CT)

Order this book online at **www.trafford.com**
or email orders@trafford.com

Most Trafford titles are also available at major online book retailers.

Printed in the United States of America.

ISBN: 978-1-4269-9748-8 (sc)
ISBN: 978-1-4269-9749-5 (hc)
ISBN: 978-1-4269-9750-1 (e)

Library of Congress Control Number: 2011918139

Trafford rev. 10/12/2011

 www.trafford.com

North America & International
toll-free: 1 888 232 4444 (USA & Canada)
phone: 250 383 6864 ♦ fax: 812 355 4082

Contents

PREFACE

My journey began when I decide to write my own commentary on the book of Revelation. I thought I would just bypass the whole rapture debate. I would have written with a pre-tribulation rapture belief.

Then I debated with my pastor on a different point of eschatology. He asked me about my position on the day of the Lord. He had me. I just assumed it started with the rapture. I never gave the concept too much thought.

My pastor lent me the book, "The Pre-wrath Rapture of the Church," by Marvin Rosenthal. I told my pastor it was a great read, and it made me think about the day of the Lord and a lot of other issues. But I was not convinced and I told him so. Over the months I read many different rapture books (mostly pre-tribulation positions), the Bible, and Marvin Rosenthal's book a couple of more times.

Months later, I went back to my pastor and told him that I no longer believed in the pre-tribulation rapture. I believed in the Pre-wrath rapture. I still had skepticism. I wanted to believe in a pre-tribulation rapture. But I continued to study more and more. I sometimes studied three to four hours a night on a work night.

The whole rapture debate centers on where one believes the day of the Lord begins in relationship to Daniel's seventieth week. Most eschatologists do agree that the rapture and the day of the Lord do occur together. Some believe the day of the Lord begins at the rapture while the other side believes the day of the Lord follows closely behind the rapture. Most agree there is an intimate relationship between the two.

The pre-tribulation rapture position mostly has the beginning of the day of the Lord begin with the confirming of a covenant with many.

The pre-wrath rapture has the day of the Lord beginning between the abomination of desolation and Armageddon.

The post tribulation rapture has the day of the Lord beginning at the end of Daniel's seventieth week following the cosmic disturbance of Matthew 24:29.

It became increasingly clear that the rapture takes place at the end of Daniel's seventieth week.

Once your mind has a certain idea about some belief or issue, it is hard to go against what you believe to be true. We tend to ignore or skip over information which is contradictory to what we think is right.

When our mind is taught something and we believe it is true, it is difficult to grasp that the idea may be wrong. We either ignore the data that is against what we hold true, or we investigate it further. Most of the time, we ignore that which opposes our own thoughts and belief systems.

I once believed in a pre-tribulation rapture (The rapture occurring before the confirming of the covenant with many which begins the seventieth week of Daniel-more commonly known as the tribulation period).

I now believe in the post-tribulation rapture (The rapture occurring at the end of the seventieth week of Daniel). I will now try to lay out the evidence to you.

I have tried not to take shots at the pre-tribulation rapture position. I have tried to only highlight the beliefs associated with that position. I believe the men who have written the commentaries and books that hold to the pre-tribulation rapture position to be men of God. I just believe they are wrong on this issue.

All Biblical references used in this book are from the Oxford NIV Schofield Study Bible (1984 edition) unless otherwise noted.

Scott A. Wheeler

Special thanks to my wife and kids for putting up with me. Many thanks go to my friend Joe Griffin for editing and listening to me.

Section 1

Introduction to Concepts

This section, the first five chapters will cover definitions and explanations of some of the eschatological themes found in this book. This section will cover the topics of what is a rapture, why is there a rapture, the day of the Lord and its' relationship to the rapture, and the seventieth week of Daniel (commonly called the tribulation period).

CHAPTER 1

What is the Rapture?

The word rapture does not occur in the Bible.

We take the words "caught up" from 1 Thess 4:17, and transform them into the word "rapture."

The term "caught up" from 1 Thess 4:13 comes from the Greek word "harpazo." The definition of "harpazo" is given below.

1. To seize, carry off by force
2. To seize on, claim one's self eagerly
3. To snatch out or away [1]

The Greek scriptures were translated into Latin. The Greek word "harpazo" was translated into the Latin word "rapere." "Rapere" is where we get the English word "rapture."

The rapture is a worldwide gathering of the saints (a saint is one who has accepted Jesus as his savior). The saints will be caught up (raptured, seized or snatched away) to meet the Lord in the clouds. This worldwide gathering of the saints occurs in the twinkling of an eye (in other words instantly). The saints who have been caught up (raptured) to meet Jesus in the air shall have their bodies transformed from the mortal to the immortal. Our bodies will be similar to Jesus' glorified body.

The righteous dead are also raised at the time of the rapture. The righteous dead will have their bodies raised from the grave. Their bodies

---

[1] Strong's Number Reference from the Word Bible Collection CD, 2006

will also be immortal, imperishable just like those saints who have been raptured.

The rapture event is in this order. The Lord will come down from Heaven. There will be a loud command, a shout of the archangel, and the trumpet call of God. The dead will be raised and receive an immortal body. The saints who are alive and left at the second coming of Jesus will be caught up to Jesus along with the righteous dead and meet the Lord in the air. The saints who are alive at the second coming of Jesus shall also receive an immortal body. They will be with the Lord forever.

There are two rapture passages that most eschatologists (one who studies the last days) agree on that deal with the rapture. The two rapture passages are 1 Thessalonians 4:13-18 and 1 Corinthians 15:51-52. These passages are given below.

Brothers, we do not want you to be ignorant about those who fall asleep, or to grieve like the rest of men, who have no hope. We believe that Jesus died and rose again and so we believe that God will bring with Jesus those who have fallen asleep in him. According to the Lord's own word, we tell you that we who are still alive, who are left till the coming of the Lord, will certainly not precede those who have fallen asleep. For the Lord himself will come down from heaven, with a loud command, with the voice of the archangel and with the trumpet call of God, and the dead in Christ will rise first. After that, we who are still alive and are left will be caught up together with them in the clouds to meet the Lord in the air. And so we will be with the Lord forever. Therefore encourage each other with these words.

1 Thessalonians 4:13-18

Listen, I tell you a mystery: We will not all sleep, but we will all be changed—in a flash, in the twinkling of an eye, at the last trumpet. For the trumpet will sound, the dead will be raised imperishable, and we will be changed.

1 Corinthians 15:51-52

In these two rapture passages, there is no indication as to when the rapture event is to occur.

The various rapture positions connect the rapture with the day of the Lord (Day of the Lord is discussed in chapter five). It is a widely held belief that the rapture occurs at the start of the day of Lord or shortly before the day of the Lord. What the day of the Lord is and when does the day of the Lord begin, is the argument over the rapture debate. When does the day of the Lord begin? Your answer determines your rapture position.

There are two major rapture positions, but there are several more rapture opinions. Each rapture position has a unique relationship as to when the day of the Lord begins.

The first position is the pre-tribulation rapture. The term pre-tribulation rapture means that the rapture of the believers occurs before the tribulation period. The tribulation period is the seventieth week of Daniel. (The seventieth week of Daniel is discussed in chapter four)

This is the popular theory of the twentieth and twenty-first centuries. It has been brought to the forefront through both fiction and non-fiction books and movies over the last thirty plus years. Examples of these works are The Late Great Planet Earth by Hal Lindsey, and the Left Behind Series by Tim Lahaye.

There are two differing opinions as to the relationship of the day of the Lord to the rapture among those holding to the theory of a pre-tribulation rapture. The following two graphs illustrate these positions.

First Pre-tribulation Rapture theory

DOL= Day of the Lord

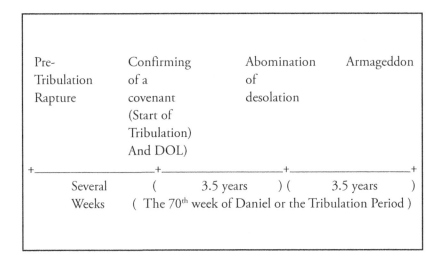

Second Pre-tribulation Rapture theory

The pre-tribulation rapture theories are basically the same. The theory maintains that no signs will precede the rapture event. At the rapture event, those who have died and accepted Jesus as their savior are raised from the dead. The righteous dead will meet the Lord in the air. Those who are still alive will be caught up to the Lord in the air. The resurrected and the living believers will have their bodies transformed into immortal bodies. Then the resurrected and those who were still alive at the time of the rapture are taken to Heaven. The believers will spend seven plus years in Heaven.

Several weeks after the rapture event (some suggest maybe a couple of months), the confirming of the covenant found in Daniel 9:25-27 takes place. This confirming of a covenant begins the seventieth week of Daniel which lasts for seven years (the pre-tribulation believer calls these last seven years the tribulation period instead of the seventieth week of Daniel).

Three and a half years into the seventieth week of Daniel, the abomination of desolation takes place.

Three and a half years later, the believers come back with Jesus to the earth. This is the end of the seventieth week of Daniel. Armageddon takes place. Jesus rules and reigns on the earth.

The pre-tribulation theories maintain that there are only two comings of Jesus. The first coming of Jesus was his birth, death, and resurrection. The second coming of Jesus is to be divided into two parts. Part 2a is to be the rapture event. Part 2b is the defeat of the enemies of God and the establishment of Jesus' kingdom on earth.

6-4 B.C.	30-33 A.D.	Rapture (7+years)	Armageddon
+			+
Birth	Death and	Part 2a of	Part 2b
Of Jesus	Resurrection	second coming	second coming
		Of Jesus	Of Jesus
		Rapture event	Rule of Jesus

The second rapture position discussed in this book is the post-tribulation rapture. This is the position of this book. As the name of the position conveys, this position has the rapture occurring at the end of the seventieth week of Daniel.

The post-tribulation rapture theory believes in only one second coming of Jesus. At the end of the seventieth week of Daniel, Jesus, God, and the angels come down from Heaven. The rapture event transpires. The righteous dead, both the Old Testament saints and the New Testament saints, are resurrected and caught up to the Lord. Those saints who are still alive at the second coming of Jesus shall also be caught up to meet the Lord. All of the saints now accompany Jesus back to the earth. Jesus rules and reigns on the earth.

Post-tribulation Rapture Theory

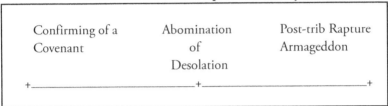

The post tribulation rapture position maintains that there are only two comings of Jesus. There are no part 2a and 2b to the second coming of Jesus. God is a God of order, not disorder.

Summary

What constitutes the day of the Lord, and when the day of the Lord begins determines a believer's rapture position. Both rapture positions assume a relationship between the rapture and the day of the Lord.

The pre-tribulation rapture position maintains that the entire seventieth week of Daniel is part of the day of the Lord. The day of the Lord begins with the confirming of the covenant with many found in Daniel 9:25-27. This position believes the church is raptured and the New Testament saints are raised from the dead shortly before the confirming of the covenant with many.

The post-tribulation rapture position holds to only one second coming of Jesus at the end of the seventieth week of Daniel. The day of the Lord begins with the return of Jesus, the resurrection of all believers, the rapture of those still alive at the coming of Christ, and the ruling and reigning of Jesus on the earth.

The pre-tribulation position has God, Jesus, and the angels come down out of Heaven to the clouds of the earth. The dead Christians are raised from the grave (the Old Testament saints are not resurrected at this time[2]). The Christians alive at the second coming of Christ are caught up to clouds along with the resurrected. Their mortal bodies are transformed into immortal bodies similar to Jesus. They all leave earth. They all travel to Heaven. They all stay in Heaven for seven plus years. They all come back to earth seven plus years later.

The post-tribulation position has God, Jesus, and the angels come down from Heaven. The righteous dead (both the Old Testament saints and New Testament saints) come forth from the grave, and are caught up to the Lord. Those Christians who are still alive at the second coming of Jesus shall be caught up (raptured) along with the dead saints. The risen saints and the saints living at the time of the rapture shall have their mortal bodies transformed into immortal bodies. The saints (all of them) will accompany God, Jesus, and the angels back to the earth. The reign of Jesus, the son of David, begins.

---

[2]   Hal Lindsey, The Rapture(New York: Bantam Books,1983), 192

CHAPTER 2

Why a Rapture?

The Bible never gives a reason for why there is a rapture. The Bible never specifically states, "There will be a rapture because of such and such."

The day of the Lord is a great, glorious, and dreadful day according to Acts 2:20 and Joel 3:31. The reason for a rapture may be the escape of the believers from the dreadful part of the day of the Lord. The great and glorious part is the return of Jesus. The dreadful part is the punishment of the unrighteous (those who deny Jesus as their savior).

Paul is the author of First and Second Thessalonians. These two books of the Bible were letters. These letters were written by Paul to the Christian believers in the city of Thessalonica. These letters (1 & 2 Thess) were written by Paul for the encouragement of the people of Thessalonica, and to explain and expound upon some of the teachings Paul gave to the Thessalonians. It is estimated that Paul only spent anywhere from one to six months teaching and preaching in Thessalonica due to persecution.[3]

Even though Paul only spent a small amount of time in in Thessalonica, he seemed to have gone into depth on several matters including eschatology. The believers in Thessalonica may have been concerned about those who had already died in Christ. Would the dead still be part of the second coming of Jesus? This may have been a question posed to Paul from the people of Thessalonica.

---

[3]   Charles C. Ryrie, First and Second Thessalonians(Chicago: Moody Press,2001), 12

Paul may have been reassuring the saints of Thessalonica that those brothers who have already died in Christ would still be part of the second coming of Jesus Christ. The dead would still receive their immortal, imperishable body just as the believers who are alive and left at the second coming of Jesus Christ will have their bodies changed like Jesus' body at Jesus' appearance.

It is also held that the Thessalonians believed that they may have missed the rapture and the harsh persecutions they were enduring were part of the day of the Lord.[4]

In Paul's second letter to the Thessalonians, especially 2 Thess 2:1-4, Paul addressed the timing of the day of the Lord. It is 2 Thess 2:1-2 which associates the rapture with the day of the Lord. (Concerning the coming of our Lord Jesus Christ and our being gathered to him, we ask you, brothers, not to become easily unsettled or alarmed by some prophecy, report or letter supposed to have come from us, saying that the day of the Lord has already come.—2 Thess 2:1—) Both rapture positions (pre-tribulation and post-tribulation) associates the rapture with the day of the Lord just as Paul associated our being gathered to Jesus (the rapture) and the day of the Lord. The argument between the differing rapture positions is what the day of the Lord is.

Paul assured the Thessalonians that they had not missed the rapture. In 2 Thess, Paul told them not to be upset about some prophecy, report, or letter telling them the day of the Lord had already come. The coming of our Lord Jesus Christ and our being gathered to him (the rapture) is part of the day of the Lord.

---

[4]   Charles C. Ryrie, First and Second Thessalonians(Chicago: Moody Press,2001), 14,107

Summary

The reason for the rapture is probably the escape of the believers from the dreadful part of the day of the Lord. The believer is not to experience the harshness of the day of the Lord. This is the same belief held by the two rapture positions.

The saints are not to endure the wrath of God. God's wrath is reserved for those who reject his Son, Jesus. This may be why the saints are raptured before the dreadful part of the day of the Lord.

> *For God did not appoint us to suffer wrath but to receive salvation through our Lord Jesus Christ. He died for us so that, whether we are awake or asleep, we may live together with him.* 1 Thessalonians 5:9-10

The pre-tribulation rapture position believes that the Christian is to be spared from the seventieth week of Daniel. Even though believers were present during the first sixty-nine weeks of Daniel, this position believes that the Christians will be exempt from the seventieth week of Daniel. This position believes that the seventieth week of Daniel is part of the day of the Lord. Therefore, since this position believes that the seventieth week of Daniel is part of the day of the Lord, the Christian will be spared from the seventieth week of Daniel by a rapture. The believers go to Heaven for seven plus years. After seven plus years, the Christians come back to earth with Jesus.

The post-tribulation rapture position has God, Jesus, and the angels come down from Heaven after the seventieth week of Daniel. The rapture event occurs. Nobody goes back to Heaven. The believers accompany Jesus back to earth. The enemies of God are taken care of. Jesus rules and reigns on the earth.

CHAPTER 3

How is the Day of the Lord Associated with the Rapture?

Paul associates the rapture with the day of the Lord. This is found in both of Paul's letters to the Thessalonians specifically in 1 Thessalonians 4:13-5:11 and 2 Thessalonians 2:1-4.

Paul starts with the second coming of Jesus and the rapture (our being gathered to him). Paul wanted to reassure the Thessalonians that they had not missed the rapture for the day of the Lord had not yet come.

Paul reminded the Thessalonians that the day of the Lord/rapture will not occur until two events transpire. Those two events that occur before the day of the Lord/rapture are the rebellion (apostasy) and the man of lawlessness being revealed. (The man of lawlessness has been assumed to be the Antichrist)

> Concerning the coming of our Lord Jesus Christ and our being gathered to him, we ask you, brothers, not to become easily unsettled or alarmed by some prophecy, report or letter supposed to have come from us, saying that the day of the Lord has already come. Don't let anyone deceive you in any way, for (that day will not come) until the rebellion occurs and the man of lawlessness is revealed, the man doomed to destruction. He will oppose and will exalt himself over everything that is called God or is worshiped, so that he sets himself up in God's temple, proclaiming himself to be God. (2Thess 2:1-4)

Because the day of the Lord and the rapture are associated together by Paul, the apostasy and the revealing of the man of lawlessness must occur before the rapture.

Also In 1 Thess 4:13-5:10, Paul associates the day of the Lord with the rapture. 1 Thess 4:13-18 describes the rapture event. Chapter 5 begins with the word "now." Some commentators believe that Paul is beginning a new subject. They believe Paul finished speaking of the rapture in chapter four, and in chapter five he was moving to a new subject, the day of the Lord.

> Now(Greek word "De"), brothers, about times and dates we do not need to write to you, for you know very well that the day of the Lord will come like a thief in the night. (1 Thess 5:1-2)(Italics mine)

The Greek word "de" is translated into the words "but" or "now." "De" can be adversative or continuative. So, "de" can be used to introduce a new topic (such as going from talking about the rapture to a new topic such as the day of the Lord), or "de" (now) can be used to expound or expand a topic (such as the relationship between the day of the Lord and the rapture).

Some people believe Paul is starting a new subject (the day of the Lord), but Paul is expounding on the timing of the rapture (spoken about in 1 Thess 4:13-18) and its' relationship to the day of the Lord. The division of chapters and verses found in the Bible are man's insertions. Paul did not write a letter to the church of Thessalonica labeled with five chapters, and each chapter broken down into verses. He wrote a letter just like we write a letter today. The chapters and verses found in today's Bible are to make the Bible easy to reference to for certain verse or chapters. It also makes the Bible easier to read. Below is given the entire text of 1 Thessalonians 4:13-5:10 to show the continuity of the scriptures.

Brothers, we do not want you to be ignorant about those who fall asleep, or to grieve like the rest of men, who have no hope. We believe that Jesus died and rose again and so we believe that God will bring with Jesus those who have fallen asleep in him. According to the Lord's own word, we tell you that we who are still alive, who are left till the coming of the Lord, will certainly not precede those who have fallen asleep. For the Lord himself will come down from heaven, with a loud command, with the voice of the archangel and with the trumpet call of God, and the dead in Christ will rise first. After that, we who are still alive and are left will be caught up together with them in the clouds to meet the Lord in the air. And so we will be with the Lord forever. Therefore encourage each other with these words.

Now ("De", this is 1 Thess 5:1), brothers, about times and dates we do not need to write to you, for you know very well that the day of the Lord will come like a thief in the night. While people are saying, "Peace and safety," destruction will come on them suddenly, as labor pains on a pregnant woman, and they will not escape.

But you, brothers, are not in darkness so that this day should surprise you like a thief. You are all sons of the light and sons of the day. We do not belong to the night or to the darkness. So then, let us not be like others, who are asleep, but let us be alert and self-controlled. For those who sleep, sleep at night, and those who get drunk, get drunk at night. But since we belong to the day, let us be self-controlled, putting on faith and love as a breastplate, and the hope of salvation as a helmet. For God did not appoint us to suffer wrath but to receive salvation through our Lord Jesus Christ. He died for us so that, whether we are awake or asleep, we may live together with him. (1 Thess 4:13-5:10)

In 1 Thess 5:1, Paul is continuing on the subject of the rapture and the relationship between the rapture and the day of the Lord. Paul goes on to explain how we do not need to know about times and dates (similar to the Lord's teaching in Matt 24:36, "No one knows about that day or hour." Paul puts the day of the Lord along with the rapture saying, "that the day of the Lord will come like a thief in the night." In his second letter to the Thessalonians 2:1-2, Paul again puts our being gathered to Jesus at his coming and warning the people that the day of the Lord has not come. In 2 Thess 2:3-4, Paul states the day of the Lord will not occur until the rebellion (apostasy) and the man of lawlessness is revealed. So, there is a relationship between the rapture and the day of the Lord.

It is important to note that Paul in 1 Thess 5 does not state that the day of the Lord will take the believer by surprise. Only the unbeliever will be taken by surprise at the coming of Jesus. The Christian is to know the signs preceding the second coming of Jesus. (Such as the apostasy and the revealing of the man of lawlessness)

The day of the Lord will come like a thief in the night to the unbeliever. The believer will know the general timing of the day of the Lord. And the day of the Lord is associated with the rapture according to Paul. So the rapture will not occur until after the apostasy, and the revealing of the man of lawlessness.

In both of Paul's letters to the Thessalonians, Paul associates the day of the Lord with the rapture.

Summary

Each rapture position associates the day of the Lord with the rapture event. Below are given the two pre-tribulation rapture position timelines.

First Pre-tribulation Rapture theory

Pre-Tribulation Rapture (Start of DOL)	Confirming of a covenant (Start of Tribulation)	Abomination of desolation	Armageddon

+_____+_____+_____+

Several Weeks   (3.5 years   ) (3.5 years   )

(The 70th week of Daniel or the Tribulation Period)

Second Pre-tribulation Rapture theory

Pre-Tribulation Rapture	Confirming of a covenant (Start of Tribulation And DOL)	Abomination of desolation	Armageddon

+_____+_____+_____+

Several Weeks   (3.5 years   ) (3.5 years   )

(The 70th week of Daniel or the Tribulation Period)

DOL=Day of the Lord

For the pre-tribulation rapture position to be Biblically coherent, the apostasy and the revealing of the man of lawlessness must occur before their respective days of the Lord. Paul associates the day of the Lord with the rapture, therefore, the apostasy and revealing of the man of lawlessness occurs before the rapture.

Post-tribulation Rapture Theory

Confirming of a Covenant	Abomination of Desolation	Post-trib Rapture Armageddon DOL
+_____+_____		
(70th week of Daniel)		
DOL= Day of the Lord		

The post-tribulation rapture is Biblically coherent. In this position both the apostasy and the revealing of the man of lawless can occur before the rapture and the day of the Lord.

CHAPTER 4

What is the Seventieth Week of Daniel?

The seventieth week of Daniel is most commonly called the tribulation period even though the Bible never says that. The only use of the word tribulation is seen in Rev 7:14 where it is described as the great tribulation. Most commentators who use the term, "the tribulation period," call the last three and a half years the great tribulation. And the whole seven year period they call the tribulation. Again, the Bible never calls the last seven years the tribulation period. The last seven years are the seventieth week of Daniel.

Confirming of a Covenant	Abomination of Desolation	Armageddon
+_____+_____+		
(3.5 years)(	3.5 years	)
Tribulation	Great Tribulation	
(Whole Tribulation Period lasting seven years		)

Gabriel the angel spoke to Daniel and gave him the message found in Daniel 9:24-27. This is where we get the seventy weeks of Daniel.

"Seventy 'sevens' are decreed for your people and your holy city to finish transgression, to put an end to sin, to atone for wickedness, to bring in everlasting righteousness, to seal up vision and prophecy and to anoint the most holy.

"Know and understand this: "From the issuing of the decree to restore and rebuild Jerusalem until the Anointed One, the ruler, comes, there will be seven 'sevens,' and sixty-two 'sevens.' It will be rebuilt with streets and a trench, but in times of trouble. After the sixty-two 'sevens,' the Anointed One will be cut off and will have nothing. The people of the ruler who will come will destroy the city and the sanctuary. The end will come like a flood: War will continue until the end, and desolations have been decreed. He will confirm a covenant with many for one 'seven.' In the middle of the 'seven' he will put an end to sacrifice and offering. And on a wing *of the temple* he will set up an abomination that causes desolation, until the end that is decreed is poured out on him. (Daniel 9:24-27)

Daniel was told that "seventy sevens" were decreed to his people (Israel) and the holy city (Jerusalem) to finish transgression, to put an end to sin, to atone for wickedness, to bring in everlasting righteousness, to seal up vision and prophecy and to anoint the most holy. All of the above will be fulfilled at the second coming of Jesus! But what are the seventy sevens?

Each seven is a week of years.
One seven equals seven years.
There are seventy sevens.
This means 70 times seven years.
This makes a total of 490 years.
In 490 years, Jesus will reign on the earth.
The countdown began around 445 B.C.
Artaxerexes gave the decree to rebuild in 445 B.C. Reference found in Nehemiah 2.
But, in Daniel 9:25-26, sixty-nine sevens occur and the Messiah (Anointed One) is cut off.
483 years passed after the decree in 445 B.C.
Sometime around 30-33 A.D., Jesus ascended to Heaven
This ended the 483 years.

Jesus did not leave in the mathematical 38 A.D. (445 B.C. years and 38 years of A.D. would equal the 483 years.) We have miss-calculated our calendars. The actual birth period of Jesus is dated around 2-6 B.C.

There is another abnormality in this equation. The Jewish calendar only contained 360 days, not the current 365 days. Putting these factors together gives us the estimate of 30-33 A.D. as the cutting off of the Anointed One (Jesus).

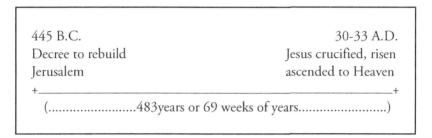

445 B.C.   30-33 A.D.
Decree to rebuild   Jesus crucified, risen
Jerusalem   ascended to Heaven

(......................483years or 69 weeks of years......................)

There is one more seven to go.

This is Daniel's seventieth week.

Daniel's seventieth week will last seven years. (Also known as the tribulation)

Daniel's seventieth week begins with the confirming of the covenant with many.

This covenant is for seven years.

The Gentiles and the Jews have comprised the church since Pentecost. Both Gentile and Jew were present for the first sixty-nine weeks (483 years), which began around 445 B.C. and lasted to around 30-33 A.D. There is one more week to go for everyone. There is one more period of seven years to go. This is the seventieth week of Daniel.

Israel rejected Jesus as the Messiah. Israel's heart has been hardened. Israel has experienced a hardening in part until the full number of the Gentiles has come in. And so all Israel will be saved. (Romans 11:25-26) The full number of Gentiles will not be complete until the second coming of Jesus at the end of Daniel's seventieth week. Revelation chapter seven tells us that people from every tribe, nation, and language will have washed their robes in the blood of the lamb, and have come out of the great tribulation. Both Jews and Gentiles who belong to the Lamb will come out of the great tribulation.

Again, everyone, Jew and Gentile alike have one more "seven" to go. Everyone has seven years to go before the return of the Messiah, Jesus. That "seven" begins with the confirming of the covenant with many.

Signing of The covenant	Abomination of Desolation	Day of the Lord
+..+..+		
3.5 years		3.5 years
(..7 Years..)		
Daniel's 70th week		

Also, the first sixty-nine weeks (483 years) started while the Jews were already under the times of the Gentiles. The times of the Gentiles began around 586 B.C. (This was when Nebuchadnezzar destroyed Jerusalem and the temple), and the Time of the Gentiles will continue through the seventieth week of Daniel. (Rev 11 and Luke 21:24) There is no scriptural evidence to say that the church will not be present during Daniel's seventieth week.

Also, it must be noted, in Revelation 12:14, Israel is protected or taken care of for the last three and half years of the seventieth week. Satan, knowing that his time is short went after Israel, but this attack will fail. So, Satan goes after those who hold to the testimony of Jesus.

Christians will be present during the seventieth week of Daniel. The church will live on. Christian and Jew have one more week to go.

Summary

The seventieth week of Daniel is the last seven years of human history before Jesus comes back to rule and reign on the earth. The seventieth week of Daniel begins with a confirming of a covenant with many.

We do not know the details about this covenant. Any guess to what the confirming of the covenant involves is just an assumption.

The world and the church may not even realize the confirming of the covenant is taking place. Ancient Israel did not start counting down the arrival of the Anointed One (Jesus) when Artaxerexes issued a decree to rebuild Jerusalem. There is no mention in the Bible or other historical documents that the Israelites went around stating, "The seventy weeks of Daniel has begun!" or "483 more years to the Anointed One (Messiah)!"

History may repeat itself. The confirming of a covenant with many may not be highly touted in the media. The confirming of a covenant with many may go unnoticed by the average person.

But the abomination of desolation will take place around the middle of the seventieth week of Daniel according to Daniel. Paul, Mark, and Matthew also speak of the desecration of God's temple by the man of lawlessness. For the believer, the abomination of desolation will probably be a clearer sign than the confirming a covenant with many. Both events take place in the seventieth week of Daniel.

First is the confirming of the covenant with many. This is the beginning of the seventieth week of Daniel.

Second is the abomination of desolation which takes place around the middle of the seventieth week of Daniel.

At the end of the seventieth week of Daniel, Jesus will rapture his church, destroy the armies at Armageddon, and establish his kingdom on earth.

CHAPTER 5

What is the Day of the Lord?

What is the day of the Lord? That is the answer to rapture question. Both rapture positions have a different opinions as to what the day of the Lord is and what is include in the day of the Lord.

The pre-tribulation rapture position believes the day of the Lord includes the rapture, the seventieth week of Daniel, and the day Jesus returns to the earth to set up his kingdom.

The other pre-tribulation rapture position believes the day of the Lord begins after the rapture. The day of the Lord begins with the confirming of a covenant, and it includes the seventieth week of Daniel and the day Jesus returns to rule over the earth.

The post-tribulation rapture position believes the day of the Lord begins with the day Jesus returns. This position only holds to one second coming of Jesus (The pre-tribulation rapture positions each have a two part second coming of Jesus-One for the rapture and the other for establishment of the kingdom of Christ on the earth). The first event in the return of Jesus is the rapture event, then

> There are various beliefs surrounding the relationship of the day of the Lord with the millennial rule of Jesus (the 1,000 year reign of Jesus on the earth found in Rev.20.) Each rapture position has varying opinions within each position as whether or not to include the millennial rule of Jesus as part of the day of the Lord. This argument is not fleshed out in this book.

the destruction of the armies of the Anti-Christ, and the rule and reign of Jesus on the earth.

It is best to allow the scriptures to explain what the day of the Lord is. The day of the Lord is referenced to as the day of the Lord, that day, day of God's wrath, day of his coming, and day of our Lord Jesus Christ. Some of the verses have been shortened to focus in on the aspects of the day of the Lord to make it an easier reading. Given below are the following verses which contain references to the day of the Lord.

Elijah comes before the great and dreadful day of the Lord-Malachi 4:5

The day of the Lord is great; it is dreadful. Who can endure it?—Joel 2:11

Woe to you who long for the day of the Lord! Why do you long for the day of the Lord? That day will be darkness, not light. It will be as though a man fled from a lion only to meet a bear, as though he entered his house and rested his hand on the wall only to have a snake bite him. Will not the day of the Lord be darkness, not light—pitch-dark, without a ray of brightness?-Amos 5:18-20

The sun will be turned to darkness and the moon to blood <u>before</u> the coming of the day of the Lord-Acts 2:20 and Joel 2:31

The sun turned black, the moon blood red, the stars fell, the sky receded like a scroll, mountains and islands removed from its place, men hide in caves and call on the rocks to fall on them for the day of God's wrath has come (or is about to begin)-Rev 6:12

The rising sun will be darkened-Isaiah 13:10

The moon will not give its light-Isaiah 13:10

The stars of heaven and their constellations will not show their light-Isaiah 13:10

All the stars of the heavens will be dissolved and the sky rolled up like a scroll; all the starry hosts will fall-Isaiah 34:4

That day will bring about the destruction of the heavens by fire and the elements will melt in the heat-2 Peter 3:10

Men will flee to caves in the rocks and to holes in the ground from dread of the Lord and the splendor of his majesty, when he rises to shake the earth—Isaiah 2:10, 19

Alas for that day! For the day of the LORD is near; it will come like destruction from the Almighty.—Joel 1:15

Be silent before the Sovereign Lord, for the day of the Lord is near-Zephaniah 1:7

The Lord alone will be exalted in that day—Isaiah 2:11

Men will be brought low; they will be humbled—Isaiah 2:11

Wail for the day of the Lord is near; it will come like destruction from the Almighty—Isaiah 13:6

The day of the Lord is near; it will come like destruction from the Almighty-Joel 1:15

Men's hearts will melt; terror will seize them; they will look aghast at each other, their faces aflame—Isaiah 13:7-8

The day of the Lord is coming—a cruel day, with wrath and fierce anger—to make the land desolate and destroy the sinner within it—Isaiah 13:9

God will punish the world for its evil, the wicked for their sins—Isaiah 13:11

Man will be scarcer than pure gold—Isaiah 13:12

Therefore I will make the heavens tremble; and the earth will shake from its place at the wrath of the Lord Almighty, in the day of his burning anger—Isaiah 13:13

Suddenly, in an instant, the Lord Almighty will come with thunder and earthquake and great noise, with windstorm and tempest and flames of a devouring fire.—Isaiah 29:5

Seventh bowl-Lightning, rumblings, peals of thunder, a severe earthquake, every island fled away and mountains could not be found, 100 pound hailstones—Rev 16:17-21

Sixth seal—sky recedes like a scroll, every mountain and island removed from its place, sun black, moon blood red—Rev 6:12-14

Seventh trumpet—Flashes of lightning, rumblings, peals of thunder, an earthquake, and a great hailstorm-Rev 11:19

On that day there will be no light, no cold or frost-it will be a unique day, without daytime or nighttime—a day known to the Lord-Zech 14:6

The cry on the day of the Lord will be bitter, the shouting of the warrior there. That day will be a day of wrath, distress, anguish, trouble, ruin, darkness, gloom, clouds, blackness, trumpet, and battle cry against the fortified cities—Zephaniah 1:14-16

The Lord is angry with all nations; his wrath is upon all their armies. He will totally destroy them, he will give them over to slaughter—Isaiah 34:2

For the Lord has a day of vengeance, a year of retribution, to uphold Zion's cause—Isaiah 34:8

For the day of vengeance was in my heart, and the year of my redemption has come—Isaiah 63:4

How awful that day will be! None will be like it. It will be a time of trouble for Jacob, but he will be saved out of it. "'In that day,' declares the Lord Almighty, 'I will break the yoke off their necks and will tear off their bonds; no longer will foreigners enslave them. Instead, they will serve the LORD their God and David their king, whom I will raise up for them."—Jeremiah 30:7-9

Blow the trumpet, sound the alarm on my holy hill. Let all who live in the land tremble for the day of the Lord is coming. It is close at hand-A day of darkness and gloom, a day of clouds, and blackness. A large and mighty army comes-such as never was or will be—a fire devours everything. At the sight of the army, the nations are in anguish-every face turns pale. Before the army is the Lord and his forces are beyond number. The earth shakes; the sky trembles, the sun, moon, and stars are darkened.—Joel 2:1-11

Whoever flees at the sound of terror will fall into a pit; whoever climbs out of the pit will be caught in a snare. The floodgates of the heavens are opened, the foundations of the earth shake. The earth is broken up, the earth is split asunder, the earth is thoroughly shaken. The earth reels like a drunkard, it sways like a hut in the wind; so heavy upon it is the guilt of its rebellion that it falls—never to rise again. In that day the LORD will punish the powers in the heavens above and the kings on the earth below. They will be herded together like prisoners bound in a dungeon; they will be shut up in prison and be punished after many days. The moon will be abashed, the sun ashamed; for the LORD Almighty will reign on Mount Zion and in Jerusalem, and before its elders, gloriously.—Isaiah 24:18-23

Then they gathered the kings together to the place that in Hebrew is called Armageddon-Revelation 16:16

Therefore wait for me," declares the LORD, "for the day I will stand up to testify. I have decided to assemble the nations, to gather the kingdoms and to pour out my wrath on them—all my fierce anger. The whole world will be consumed by the fire of my jealous anger."—Zephaniah 3:8

Swing the sickle, for the harvest is ripe. Come, trample the grapes, for the winepress is full and the vats overflow—so great is their wickedness!"-Joel 3:13

The angel swung his sickle on the earth, gathered its grapes and threw them into the great winepress of God's wrath. They were trampled in the winepress outside the city, and blood flowed out of the press, rising as high as the horses' bridles for a distance of 1,600 stadia (about 180 miles).—Revelation 14:19-20

Multitudes, multitudes in the valley of decision! For the day of the LORD is near in the valley of decision.

The sun and moon will be darkened, and the stars no longer shine. The LORD will roar from Zion and thunder from Jerusalem; the earth and the sky will tremble. But the LORD will be a refuge for his people, a stronghold for the people of Israel.—Joel 3:14-16

"Son of man, prophesy and say 'This is what the Sovereign LORD says: "'Wail and say, "Alas for that day!" For the day is near, the day of the LORD is near—a day of clouds, a time of doom for the nations."—Ezekiel 30:2-3

On that day,
Jerusalem will be an immovable rock
Horses will be blind and panic-riders struck with madness
Jerusalem will be intact
The Lord will shield those who live in Jerusalem
The Lord will destroy all nations that attack Jerusalem
Weeping and mourning in Jerusalem will be great
Banishment of idols and removal of both prophets and the spirit of impurity from the Lord
Jesus' feet will stand on the Mount of Olives
Mount of Olives split in two, a great valley is formed
All the holy ones will be with him
No light
No cold or frost
No daytime or nighttime
When evening comes there will be light
Living water will flow out from Jerusalem
Men will be stricken with great panic
Men will attack each other
Men's flesh will rot while they are standing on their feet, their eyes will rot in their sockets, and their tongues will rot in their mouths-Zechariah 12-14

But who can endure the day of his coming? Who can stand when he appears? For he will be like a refiner's fire or a launderer's soap. He will sit as a refiner and purifier of silver; he will purify the Levites and refine them like gold and silver. Then the LORD will have men who will bring offerings in righteousness-Malachi 3:2-3

"'In the whole land," declares the LORD, "two-thirds will be struck down and perish; yet one-third will be left in it. This third I will bring into the fire; I will refine them like silver and test them like gold. They will call on my name and I will answer them; I will say, 'They are my people,' and they will say, 'The LORD' is our God.'"-Zechariah 13:8-9

Surely the day is coming; it will burn like a furnace. All the arrogant and every evildoer will be stubble, and that day that is coming will set them on fire," says the LORD Almighty. "Not a root or a branch will be left to them.—Malachi 4:1

Therefore earth's inhabitants are burned up, and very few are left-Isaiah 24:6

They will make war against the Lamb, but the Lamb will overcome them because he is Lord of lords and King of kings—and with him will be his called, chosen and faithful followers-Revelation 17:14

But the day of the Lord will come like a thief.—2 Peter 3:10

"Behold, I come like a thief! Blessed is he who stays awake and keeps his clothes with him, so that he may not go naked and be shamefully exposed."-Revelation 16:15

Now, brothers, about times and dates we do not need to write to you, for you know very well that the day of the Lord will come like a thief in the night. While people are saying, "Peace and safety," destruction will come on them suddenly, as labor pains on a pregnant woman, and they will not escape. But you, brothers, are not in darkness so that this day should surprise you like a thief. You are all sons of the light and sons of the day. We do not belong to the night or to the darkness. So then, let us not be like others, who are asleep, but let us be alert and self-controlled. For those who sleep, sleep at night, and those who get drunk, get drunk at night. But since we belong to the day, let us be self-controlled, putting on faith and love as a breastplate, and the hope of salvation as a helmet. For God did not appoint us to suffer wrath but to receive salvation through our Lord Jesus Christ. He died for us so that, whether we are awake or asleep, we may live together with him-1 Thessalonians 5:1-11

Concerning the coming of our Lord Jesus Christ and our being gathered to him, we ask you, brothers, not to become easily unsettled or alarmed by some prophecy, report or letter supposed to have come from us, saying that the day of the Lord has already come. Don't let anyone deceive you in any way, for (that day will not come) until the rebellion occurs and the man of lawlessness is revealed, the man doomed to destruction. He will oppose and will exalt himself over everything that is called God or is worshiped, so that he sets himself up in God's temple, proclaiming himself to be God.—2 Thessalonians 2:1-4

Therefore you do not lack any spiritual gift as you eagerly wait for our Lord Jesus Christ to be revealed. He will keep you strong to the end, so that you will be blameless on the day of our Lord Jesus Christ. (Or the day of the Lord)-1 Corinthians 1:7-8

Being confident of this, that he who began a good work in you will carry it on to completion until the day of Christ Jesus.—Philippians 1:6

The day of the Lord is also the judgment seat of Christ-the rewarding of the believers-Philippians 2:16,1 Corinthians 3:12-15, 1 Corinthians 5:5, 1 Corinthians 5:5, 2 Timothy 4:8, 2 Corinthians 1:14, 2 Corinthians 5:10

The day of the Lord will be great, glorious, and dreadful. It is the outpouring of God's wrath on the unbelievers on earth. The saints will be raptured before the wrath of God is poured out on the earth. One third of the Israelites will survive. Throughout the rest of the earth, the inhabitants will be few. Man will be scarcer than pure gold.

There will be great panic. This will be a unique day without daytime or nighttime. When evening comes, there will be light.

A large army will come. The Lord is in front of this large and mighty army. The earth will shake and fire will devour everything. The elements will melt in the heat. Men's flesh will rot while they are standing on their feet, their eyes will rot in their sockets, and their tongues will rot in their mouths.

The kings of the earth will gather together. The Lord will assemble the nations to pour out his wrath. There will be multitudes in the valley of decision. The Lord is angry at all nations. He will destroy them. Wail and say, "Alas for that day!" For the day is near, the day of the Lord is near—a day of clouds, a time of doom for the nations.

How awful that day will be! None will be like it. It will be a time of trouble for Jacob, but he will be saved out of it. Jerusalem will be an immovable rock! The Lord will shield those who live in Jerusalem.

The blood will flow for 180 miles. The earth's inhabitants are burned up, and very few are left. It is a time of doom for the nations.

The Lord alone will be exalted. Man will be brought low.

On that day, Jesus' feet will stand on the Mount of Olives, and it will split in two. All of the holy ones will be with Jesus at his second coming.

The seventieth week of Daniel cannot be the day of the Lord. The above scriptures describing the day of the Lord do not show any indication of lasting over a seven year period. Given are three examples:

1. During the day of the Lord the stars will not show their lights. The sky will be rolled like a scroll. There will be signs on the earth and in the skies. But, during Daniel's seventieth week, the stars will be shining brightly until the fourth trumpet. At the fourth trumpet, the sun, moon and stars are struck. They will only give 2/3 of their lights. At the end of Daniel's seventieth week the stars will not show their lights.

2. During the day of the Lord, men will flee to caves to hide from the dread and the splendor of the Lord. This is unlike Daniel's seventieth week. During the seventieth week of Daniel, people will still be eating, drinking, marrying (Matthew 24:38), conducting business (Rev 18:11-19) (Rev 13:16-17) (Rev 6:6), warring (Rev 6:4), practicing their religions, etc.

3. The Lord alone will be exalted on that day. During the last half of Daniels's seventieth week, the Antichrist will be given authority over every tribe, language, and people. The Antichrist is called to be worshipped during the last forty-two months of Daniel's seventieth week, but during the day of the Lord (at the end of Daniel's seventieth week); the Lord alone will be exalted in that day. (Isaiah 2:11) It is called the day of the Lord, not the day of the Antichrist.

Summary

The seventieth week of Daniel is not part of the day of the Lord. The Antichrist is exalted during the seventieth week of Daniel. During the day of the Lord, the Lord alone will be exalted. People will be eating, drinking, marrying during the seventieth week of Daniel. During the day of the Lord people will be hiding from Jesus. The sun, moon and stars will be shining throughout most of the seventieth week of Daniel (the fourth bowl of wrath will scorch the inhabitants of earth). During the day of the Lord, there will be clouds and darkness.

There are four other events which according to the Bible occur before the day of the Lord/rapture, and they are the following.

1. The cosmic disturbance comes before the day of the Lord.
2. An Elijah comes before the day of the Lord.
3. The revealing of the Antichrist comes before the day of the Lord
4. The Apostasy comes before the day of the Lord.

These four events will be discussed in section two of this book.

The seventieth week of Daniel is not part of the day of the Lord. The day of the Lord/rapture will take place at the end of the seventieth week of Daniel.

Section 2

When is the Day of the Lord?

This section will explain the general timing of the day of the Lord and the rapture.

CHAPTER 6

The Day of the Lord Follows the Cosmic Disturbance

According to the pre-tribulation rapture position, the rapture is an imminent event. Imminence means that Christ could come at any moment, although he may not come for two thousand years.[5] No other signs or events need to take place before the rapture will happen.

The rapture and the Day of the Lord are tied intimately together by Paul in 2 Thessalonians 2:1-2. It is in these two verses where we find the coming of Jesus and the rapture (our being gathered to him) directly linked to the Day of the Lord. As has been discussed, there are two different beliefs in the pre-tribulation rapture position as to when the day of the Lord begins.

The first pre-tribulation rapture position believes that the Day of the Lord begins with the rapture of the church.[6](This position is held by John Walvoord, author of the book, The Rapture Question.) Then several weeks later the confirming of the covenant with many begins the seventieth week of Daniel.

The second pre-tribulation rapture position believes the day of the Lord begins after the rapture. It begins with the confirming of the covenant with many (the start of Daniel's seventieth week).(Tim LaHaye, Dave Crowley, J. Dwight Pentecost, and Paul Benware are pre-tribulation rapture authors who believe in this position) This position also holds to a

---

[5]   Mark Hitchcock and Thomas Ice, The Truth Behind Left Behind (Oregon: Multnomah Publishers, 2004),39

[6]   Robert Gundry, The Church and the Tribulation(Michigan: Zondervan Corporation, 1973),105

belief of a period of several weeks between the rapture and the signing of the covenant.[7](No scriptural evidence is given to support this position of a time gap between the rapture and the day of the Lord.)

Both of the pre-tribulation rapture positions overlook the cosmic disturbance of Joel 2:30-31 and Acts 2:20. The cosmic disturbance is when the sun will be darkened, and the moon to blood *before* the Day of the Lord.

Acts 2:20-The sun will be turned to darkness and the moon to blood before the coming of the great and glorious day of the Lord.

Joel 2:30-31-I will show wonders in the heavens and on the earth, blood and fire and billows of smoke. The sun will be turned to darkness and the moon to blood before the coming of the great and dreadful day of the LORD.

For the first pre-tribulation theory, the cosmic disturbance must take place before the rapture.

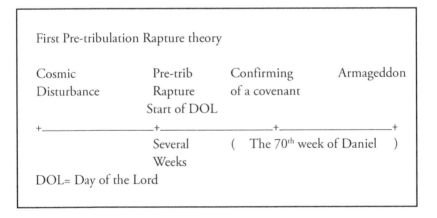

First Pre-tribulation Rapture theory

Cosmic Disturbance	Pre-trib Rapture Start of DOL	Confirming of a covenant	Armageddon
+_____	+_____	+_____	+
	Several Weeks	(The 70th week of Daniel)	

DOL= Day of the Lord

7   Hal Lindsey, The Rapture(New York: Bantam Books,1983),167

Since the cosmic disturbance must take place before the day of the Lord and the rapture is the beginning of the day of the Lord, the cosmic disturbance destroys the theory of imminence.

The second pre-tribulation theory believes the day of the Lord begins at the confirming of the covenant with many. For this theory to be scripturally accurate and hold to its' theory of imminence, a cosmic disturbance must take place between a pre-tribulation rapture and the confirming of a covenant with many.

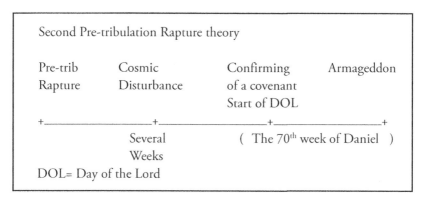

The theory of imminence (the theory of Jesus returning without any preceding events) would appear to still be viable option at this point.

The cosmic disturbance of Joel and Acts is not the only mention in the Bible of the cosmic disturbance. Joel and Acts point out that the cosmic disturbance occurs **before** the Day of the Lord. The cosmic disturbance is also mentioned in Matthew 24:29, Mark 13:24-25, and Revelation 6:12-14.

For the pre-tribulation rapture theories to be true there must be ***three cosmic disturbances!*** Pre-tribulation authors never bring this issue up in their books.

The first cosmic disturbance would occur before a pre-tribulation rapture, or after the rapture and before the signing of the covenant with many. (Refer back to the preceding graphs)

Then apparently the sky goes back to normal.

The second cosmic disturbance occurs during the seventieth week of Daniel. At the opening of the sixth seal found in Revelation 6:12-14, we find the second cosmic disturbance.

Those holding to the pre-tribulation rapture theories believe the seventh seal contains seven angels with the seven trumpets, and the seventh trumpet contains the seven angels with the seven bowls of wrath. The beliefs of these positions claim the seals, trumpets, and bowls of wrath found in the book of Revelation are sequential. So like the other cosmic disturbance, the sky will be normal again following this second cosmic disturbance.

The third cosmic disturbance would occur at the end of Daniel's seventieth week. This is found in Matthew 24:29 and Mark 13:24-25.

> I watched as he opened the sixth seal. There was a great earthquake. The sun turned black like sackcloth made of goat hair, the whole moon turned blood red, and the stars in the sky fell to earth, as late figs drop from a fig tree when shaken by a strong wind. The sky receded like a scroll, rolling up, and every mountain and island was removed from its place. (Rev 6:12-14)

> "Immediately after the distress of those days
> "'the sun will be darkened,
> and the moon will not give its light;
> the stars will fall from the sky,
> and the heavenly bodies will be shaken.' (Matt 24:29)

The following graphic illustrates what the two pre-tribulation rapture positions must look like to be in accordance with the word of God.

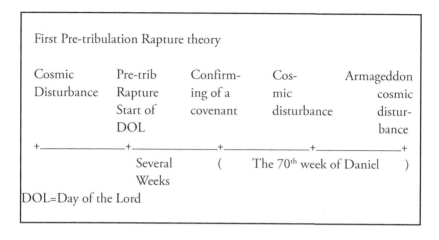

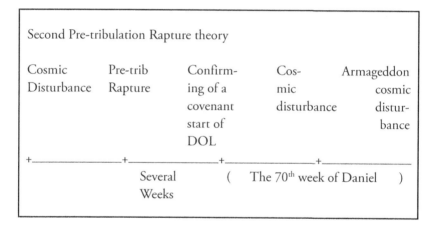

There is only one cosmic disturbance to come. The rapture cannot be a pre-tribulation rapture. This would mean that there would be three cosmic disturbances over a seven year plus period.

The rapture is a post-tribulation rapture.

The post-tribulation theory believes in one cosmic disturbance, then the Day of the Lord beginning with the rapture of the church and the destruction of the armies at Armageddon. The following graphic illustrates the position of the post-tribulation rapture theory.

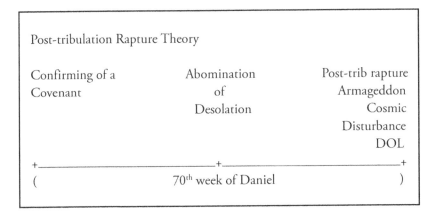

The post-tribulation rapture position believes the Acts and Joel cosmic disturbance goes along with the Matthew and Mark cosmic disturbance. And the Matthew and Mark cosmic disturbance puts the cosmic disturbance at the end of Daniel's seventieth week.

The Post-tribulation rapture does not believe the seven trumpets follow the seven seals of Revelation. And they do not believe the seven bowls follow the seven trumpets. It is believed that these events overlap.

For example, in the book of Revelation, the sixth seal is mentioned before the fourth trumpet. The sixth seal is the cosmic disturbance, and in the fourth seal one third of the sun, moon, and stars light are struck down. Another example is when the seventh trumpet sounds Jesus begins his reign and the judging of the dead has come and the rewarding of his servants has come. But there are still seven bowls of wrath to come according to the pre-tribulation position. These bowls of wrath must occur before the third woe or otherwise known as the seventh trumpet. The order of the seal, trumpets, and the bowls of wrath will be covered in chapter 14.

The sixth seal of Revelation occurs at the end of the seventieth week of Daniel.

The cosmic disturbance of the sixth seal of Revelation corresponds to cosmic disturbance of Joel, Acts, Matthew, and Mark.

Summary

The cosmic disturbance occurs at the end of Daniel's seventieth week. There is only one cosmic disturbance. The Rapture and the Day of the Lord follow the cosmic disturbance at the end of the seventieth week of Daniel.

Since the Day of the Lord does not happen until the darkening of the sun and the moon to blood red, the day of the Lord cannot be synonymous with Daniel's seventieth week. The day of the Lord follows the cosmic disturbance.

CHAPTER 7

The Day of the Lord May Follow the Coming of an Elijah

Malachi 4:5-6 states, "See, I will send you the prophet Elijah before that great and dreadful day of the Lord comes. He will turn the hearts of the fathers to their children, and the hearts of the children to their fathers; or else I will come and strike the land with a curse."

An Elijah comes before the day of the Lord.

The following is an excerpt from the book, "The Pre-wrath Rapture of the Church," by Marvin Rosenthal:

These verses of Scripture (Malachi 4:5-6) have been a cornerstone of Jewish theology for unnumbered centuries. Year after year, beginning on the fourteenth day of the Jewish month Nisan (corresponding to March/April), Jewish people the world over celebrate the feast of Passover. During the dinner (called the Seder) on the first evening of the feast, the story of the Egyptian Exodus is recounted. The prophet Elijah plays a prominent role in the festivities. A place setting is set for the prophet Elijah. A chair is kept vacant. A cup larger and more ornate than the others, called the "cup of Elijah," is placed before his setting. At one point in the ceremony, a youngster is sent to open the door with the great expectancy that Elijah will enter, sit down, drink from the cup, and announce that the Messiah is coming.[8]

But was John the Baptist an Elijah? Did an Elijah already come?

---

[8]   Marvin Rosenthal, The Pre-wrath Rapture of the Church(Tennessee: Thomas Nelson, Inc, 1990), 94

John's father was a priest named Zechariah, and his mother's name was Elizabeth. Both were descended from Aaron the brother of Moses. Both of John's parents observed the Lord's commandments and regulations blamelessly. Elizabeth was well along in years and both childless and barren.

Zechariah's priestly division was on duty. Zechariah was chosen to go into the temple of the Lord and burn incense. Those assembled together when Zechariah was burning incense, were outside praying.

An angel of the Lord appeared to Zechariah at the right side of the altar. Zechariah was scared.

Luke 1:13-17 states. (But the angel said to him: "Do not be afraid, Zechariah; your prayer has been heard. Your wife Elizabeth will bear you a son, and you are to give him the name John. He will be a joy and delight to you, and many will rejoice because of his birth, for he will be great in the sight of the Lord. He is never to take wine or other fermented drink, and he will be filled with the Holy Spirit even from birth. Many of the people of Israel will he bring back to the Lord their God. And he will go on before the Lord, in the *spirit* and *power* of Elijah, to turn the hearts of the fathers to their children and the disobedient to the wisdom of the righteous—to make ready a people prepared for the Lord.") Italics mine

Verses sixteen and seventeen state that many of the people of Israel will he (John) bring back to the Lord their God. And he will go on before the Lord, in the *spirit* and *power* of Elijah, to turn the hearts of the fathers to their children and the disobedient to the wisdom of the righteous—to make ready a people for the Lord.

John the Baptist was not physically the prophet Elijah, but Jesus testifies in Matt 11:14 that he was the Elijah to come.

In Matthew chapter seventeen, after the transfiguration of Jesus, as they were coming down the mountain, one of the disciples asked Jesus, "Why then do the teachers of the law say that Elijah must come first?" (Matt 17:10)

Jesus replied, "To be sure, *Elijah comes and will restore all things*. But I tell you, *Elijah has already come*, and they did not recognize him, but have done to him everything they wished. In the same way the Son of Man is going to suffer at their hands." Then the disciples understood that he was talking to them about John the Baptist. (Matt 17:11-13) Italics mine

John was in the *spirit* and *power* of Elijah. John led many of the people of Israel back to God. John was the Elijah to come. John was a witness for Jesus. John prepared the way for Jesus. John definitely came before the great and dreadful day of the Lord prophecy of Malachi 4:5-6.

The question left dangling is did John fulfill Malachi 4:5-6 (See, I will send you the prophet Elijah before that great and dreadful day of the LORD comes. He will turn the hearts of the fathers to their children, and the hearts of the children to their fathers; or else I will come and strike the land with a curse.) John did not completely return the hearts of the children to their fathers. Israel rejected Jesus, and almost forty years later in 70 A.D., the land was struck with a curse. The Romans destroyed Jerusalem and the temple.

Will Elijah or another like Elijah (in the spirit and the power) come again before the day of the Lord? And will this Elijah turn the hearts of the children to their fathers? Jesus stated in Matthew 17:11, "To be sure, Elijah comes and will restore all things."

Some believe Elijah is one of the two witnesses to come. (Rev 11:3-14)

The two witnesses will prophesy for 1, 260 days. They can have fire come from their mouths. They have power to stop the rain. They have power to turn the waters into blood. They can strike the earth with plagues.

When the two witnesses have finished, the beast shall kill them. Their bodies will lie in the streets of Jerusalem. Their bodies will not be buried. The inhabitants of earth will gloat, celebrate, and send gifts to each other because these two prophets had tormented those who live on the earth.

After three and a half days, God will raise them from the dead. Terror will strike the people who see them. Then the terror stricken people will hear a loud voice from heaven saying to the witnesses, "Come up here." And the two witnesses go up to heaven in a cloud while their enemies look on. Then there will be a severe earthquake. One tenth of the city will collapse, and seven thousand people are killed.

The survivors were terrified and **gave glory** to the God of heaven. This passage is significant because throughout the rest of the Revelation mankind has continued to hide from God, curse God, and refuse to repent. This takes place in Jerusalem. Those who saw the resurrection of the two witnesses and survived the earthquake are now giving God the glory. The Jewish remnant may now be able to say, "Blessed is he who comes in the name of the Lord." This would fulfill Matthew 23:39 (For I tell you, you will not see me again until you say, "Blessed is he who comes in the name of the Lord.") The Jewish remnant may also be fulfilling Malachi 4:5-6

(See, I will send you the prophet Elijah before that great and dreadful day of the LORD comes. He will turn the hearts of the fathers to their children, and the hearts of the children to their fathers; or else I will come and strike the land with a curse.) This might also be the fulfillment of Jesus' words in Matthew 17:11, "To be sure, Elijah comes and will restore all things."

It is a widely held belief that Elijah is one of the two witnesses even though the Bible never names either witness. People have come up with all sorts of combinations of who the two witnesses will be: Elijah and Moses (because of the dispute over his body-Jude 9), Elijah and Enoch (God took him away-Genesis 5:24), Elijah and John, and several others. But what is overlooked is that John was the Elijah to come (Matt 11:14). John was in the *spirit* and *power* of Elijah not physically Elijah. (The Bible does not teach reincarnation.) Neither of the two witnesses may physically be the original Elijah, but one or both of them could be of the *power* and *spirit* of Elijah like John the Baptist was.

John the Baptist did not exhaust the prophecy of Malachi. Gabriel explained that John was Elijah in the sense that he came "in the spirit and power of Elijah" (Luke 1:17). Jesus confirmed that "Elijah is coming and will restore all things" (Matt. 17:11). This he said after John's death. An Elijah is yet to come.[9]

For the pre-tribulation rapture position to be coherent with the scriptures and their belief that the entire seven years of Daniel's seventieth week are the day of the Lord, the coming of Elijah must occur before the rapture (for those pre-tribulation believers who hold to the rapture being the start of the day of the Lord) or the coming of Elijah must occur before the signing of the covenant (for those pre-tribulation believers who hold to the signing of the covenant with many to be the beginning of the day of the Lord). Their positions would resemble the following:

---

9   Robert Gundry, The Church and the Tribulation(Michigan: Zondervan Corporation, 1973), 94

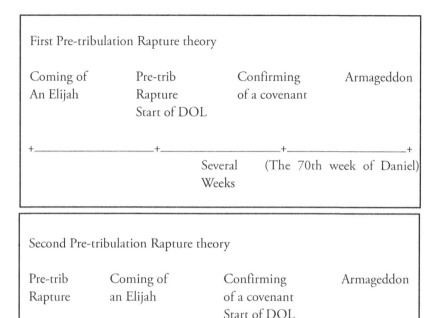

Both pre-tribulation rapture positions would have to place the coming of an Elijah before the seventieth week of Daniel. The Malachi scriptures state that an Elijah comes before the day of the Lord. Both pre-tribulation rapture positions include the entire seventieth week of Daniel as part of the day of the Lord.

Most pre-tribulation authors put the blowing of the sixth trumpet and the passing of the second woe (This corresponds to the two witnesses being called up to Heaven) past the midway point of the seventieth week of Daniel.

The two witnesses prophecy for 1,260 days. An Elijah to come may probably be one of the two witnesses.

If an Elijah comes before the pre-tribulation rapture or before the confirming of a covenant with many, Elijah's ministry will be over before the abomination of desolation which takes place around the middle of the seventieth week of Daniel. Then the Elijah could not be one of the two witnesses because the blowing of the seventh trumpet occurs in the second half of the seventieth week of Daniel according the pre-tribulation rapture position.[10]

The coming of an Elijah with the ending of his ministry near the end of the seventieth week of Daniel fits nicely with the post-tribulation rapture position.

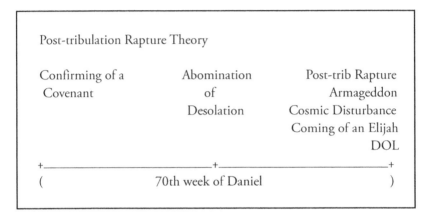

Post-tribulation Rapture Theory

| Confirming of a Covenant | Abomination of Desolation | Post-trib Rapture Armageddon Cosmic Disturbance Coming of an Elijah DOL |

```
+_____+_____+
(              70th week of Daniel              )
```

Summary

An Elijah comes before the day of the Lord. If an Elijah is one of the two witnesses, his going back to heaven occurs with passing of the second woe (the sixth trumpet blast). The second woe occurs late in Daniel's seventieth week, and the two witnesses are on the scene for only 1,260 days. The day of the Lord cannot be synonymous with Daniel's seventieth week. The day of the Lord follows the coming of an Elijah.

---

[10]   Hal Lindsey, The Rapture(New York: Bantam Books,1983),106

CHAPTER 8

The Day of the Lord Follows the Revealing of the Man of Lawlessness

Concerning the coming of our Lord Jesus Christ and our being gathered to him, we ask you, brothers, not to become easily unsettled or alarmed by some prophecy, report or letter supposed to have come from us, saying that the day of the Lord has already come. Don't let anyone deceive you in any way, for that day will not come until the rebellion occurs and the man of lawlessness is revealed, the man doomed to destruction. He will oppose and will exalt himself over everything that is called God or is worshiped, so that he sets himself up in God's temple, proclaiming himself to be God. (2 Thess 2:1-4)

It is clear from these verses that the day of the Lord follows the revealing of the man of lawlessness. (The man of lawlessness is the Antichrist to come.)

The pre-tribulation rapture position puts the revealing of the Antichrist at the signing of the covenant with many.[11]

It has been popularized that the Antichrist is going to sign a big peace treaty with Israel, but the Bible never says this. It only mentions a confirming of a covenant with many. No specific details are given. A peace treaty has just been speculation. One must stay within the boundaries of scripture and not wander into imaginations and speculations which would lead to false conclusions.

---

[11] Charles C. Ryrie, First and Second Thessalonians(Chicago: Moody Press,2001), 110

Just because the confirming of a covenant begins the seventieth week of Daniel, does not mean this will be a big earth shaking event. Remember the beginning of the first sixty-nine weeks of Daniel was not a big spectacle to the world. The start of the seventy weeks of Daniel can be found in Nehemiah 2:5. Neither the world nor the Jews went around saying, "This is it! The seventy weeks of Daniel has begun!"

The only evidence given to the revealing of the man of lawlessness was given in the scriptures at the beginning of this chapter. (2 Thess 2:1-4) This is the abomination of desolation. The Antichrist sets himself up in God's temple. He proclaims himself to be God. The revealing of the Antichrist may not occur until around the midpoint of Daniel's seventieth week.

It is at the midpoint of the seventieth week of Daniel that the abomination of desolation takes place.

The proof is found in Daniel 9:27, "He will confirm a covenant with many for one 'seven.' In the *middle* of the 'seven' he will put an end to sacrifice and offering. And on a wing of the temple he will set up an abomination that causes desolation, until the end that is decreed is poured out on him." (Emphasis mine)

It is at the abomination of desolation where the revealing of who the man of lawlessness (Antichrist) is. And this revealing of the Antichrist occurs somewhere around the middle of the seventieth week of Daniel. And the Day of the Lord follows the revealing of the Antichrist. And the Day of the Lord is connected with the rapture. So the rapture cannot occur before the Antichrist is revealed with his sitting in the temple of Jerusalem proclaiming himself to be God.

A Case in Logical Thinking

A=Rapture
B=Day of the Lord
C=Revealing of the Man of Lawlessness

(A)(B)=AB (Rapture/Day of the Lord begin at the same time)

According to 2 Thessalonians 2:3, **C** (The Revealing of the Man of Lawlessness) comes before **B** (Day of the Lord)

B (Day of the Lord) begins at the same time as **A** (Rapture)

Therefore,

C (Revealing of the Man of Lawlessness) must also come before **A** (Rapture)

The pre-tribulation rapture position is not coherent with the Bible. Whether or not the revealing of the man of lawlessness takes place at the confirming of a covenant with many or at the abomination of desolation makes no difference for the pre-tribulation rapture position. The pre-tribulation rapture position puts the rapture before the revealing of the man of lawlessness. This is contrary to the word of God. Paul put the rapture/day of the Lord *after* the revealing of the man of lawlessness.

The pre-tribulation rapture, but . . . .

The pre-tribulation believer says,
"The church must be gone!"

The pre-tribulation rapture position believes the church must be removed before the revealing of the Antichrist, and after the revealing of the Antichrist; the day of the Lord begins.

But, 2 Thessalonians never states that the church must be removed before the revealing of the Antichrist. This pre-tribulation position comes from the following text.

(Don't you remember that when I was with you I used to tell you these things? And now you know what is holding him back, so that he may be revealed at the proper time. For the secret power of lawlessness is already at work; **but the one who now holds it back will continue to do so till _he_ is taken out of the way.** (emphasis mine) And then the lawless one will be revealed, whom the Lord Jesus will overthrow with the breath of his mouth and destroy by the splendor of his coming. The coming of the lawless one will be in accordance with the work of Satan displayed in all kinds of counterfeit miracles, signs and wonders, and in every sort of evil that deceives those who are perishing. They perish because they refused to love the truth and so be saved. For this reason God sends them a powerful delusion so that they will believe the lie and so that all will be condemned who have not believed the truth but have delighted in wickedness.) (2 Thess 2:5-12)

The following excerpt is from the book, "First and Second Thessalonians," by Charles C. Ryrie.

(That pre-tribulation argument is simply this: The restrainer is God, and the instrument of restraint is the God-indwelt church (cf. Eph. 4:6 for God indwelling; Gal 2:20 for Christ indwelling; 1 Cor. 6:19 for the Spirit indwelling). It should be remembered Christ said of the divinely indwelt and empowered church that "the gates of hell shall not prevail against it" (Matt 16:18 KJV), so we can say that this indwelt, empowered church is an adequate restraining instrument against the forces of darkness. The church will not go through any of the Tribulation because the restrainer will be removed before the Lawless One is revealed, which revelation by signing the covenant with the Jews (Dan. 9:27) begins the Tribulation period. Since the restrainer is ultimately God, and since God indwells all Christians, either He must be withdrawn from the hearts of believers while they are left on earth to go through the Tribulation, or else, when He is withdrawn, all believers are taken with Him. Since it is impossible for a believer to be "disindwelt," the only alternative is that believers too will be taken out of the way before the appearance of the Lawless One, which signals the start of the Tribulation.)[12]

---

[12]   Charles C. Ryrie, First and Second Thessalonians(Chicago: Moody Press,2001), 115-116

Mr. Ryrie just stated that the church must be gone before the revealing of the Antichrist. This is opposite of scripture. The day of the Lord and the rapture are linked together by Paul. The revealing of the man of lawlessness, according to the Bible, must happen before the day of the Lord/rapture.

The pre-tribulation rapture position holds to the following:

1. The "he" is God (or the Holy Spirit; God is triune so this is an ambiguous point)
2. The church is indwelt with the "he", and the church must be removed before the revealing of the man of lawlessness.

As much as one would like to try to stretch the idea that the Holy Spirit is the church, that is all it is a stretch. This line of thinking is straining the limits of interpretation.

What is being overlooked is the Greek word for church is "ecclesia." "Ecclesia" is feminine. The church is the bride of Christ. The church is looked at as a "she," not a "he." The church having to be removed before the revealing of the man of lawlessness rests upon an unstable foundation.

Again the pre-tribulation rapture position believes:

1. The rapture of the church occurs without any preceding events.
2. They believe the church is the "he." (Despite "ecclesia" being feminine)
3. The "he" (church) is removed through the rapture.
4. The Antichrist is revealed through the signing of the covenant with many.
5. The signing of the covenant with many is the beginning of Daniel's seventieth week.
6. The signing of the covenant is what they hold to being the start of the day of the Lord.

But, the "he" is never removed.

The "he" is never removed. This is just an assumption.

The "he" has been assumed as many persons or things such as the Holy Spirit, Michael the archangel, Satan, and government to name a few. The Holy Spirit is believed to be the "he" more than any of the other theories. Again, the Bible never directly says who "he" is.

"For the secret power of lawlessness is already at work; but the one who now holds it back will continue to do so till **he** is taken out of the way." The Bible does not say until he is removed. He is taken out of the way. The New Living Translation puts it, "For this lawlessness is already at work secretly, and it will remain secret until the one who is holding it back *steps* out of the way."

Other translations are given to show there is no removal, but only a taking out of the way.

For the secret power of lawlessness is already at work; but the one who now holds it back will continue to do so till he is taken out of the way. (TNIV)

For the mystery of iniquity doth already work: only he who now letteth will let, until he be taken out of the way. (KJV)

For the mystery of lawlessness is already at work; only he who now restrains will do so until he is taken out of the way. (NASB)

The one who is now holding back the secret power of lawlessness will continue to do so until he steps or is taken out of the way. Then the man of lawlessness will be revealed, and our Lord Jesus will overthrow him at his coming.

The church does not have to be raptured before the revealing of the man of lawlessness. Scripture teaches the opposite. It teaches that the Antichrist will be revealed at the abomination of desolation. After this the Antichrist is revealed, the day of the Lord will follow. The length of time between the revealing and the day of the Lord is not given. But by putting the revealing of the Antichrist at the abomination of desolation and the day of the Lord at the end of the seventieth week of Daniel, this puts an estimated time of about three and one half years between the revealing of the Antichrist and the day of the Lord.

The pre-tribulation rapture position believes the Christian will not be here when the day of the Lord begins. Their argument goes as such: The Christian will not be surprised by the day of the Lord because the Christian will have been raptured several weeks prior to the day of the Lord. (Their belief being the day of the Lord begins with the signing of the covenant with many and this is the revealing of the Antichrist.)

But this is not what Paul taught.

(Now, brothers, about times and dates we do not need to write to you, for you know very well that the day of the Lord will come like a thief in the night. While people are saying, "Peace and safety," destruction will come on them suddenly, as labor pains on a pregnant woman, and they will not escape.

But you, brothers, are not in darkness so that this day should surprise you like a thief. You are all sons of the light and sons of the day. We do not belong to the night or to the darkness. So then, let us not be like others, who are asleep, but let us be alert and self-controlled.) (1 Thess 5:1-6)

But you, brothers, are not in darkness so that this day (the day of the Lord) should surprise you like a thief. The sons of the light (Christians) will be here when the signing of the covenant takes place and during Daniel's seventieth week.

The pre-tribulation rapture believer needs to answer the question. If you are raptured before the man of lawlessness is revealed (the beginning of the day of the Lord for the per-tribulation believer), why would Paul say the day of the Lord will not be a surprise to the believer?

The answer is simple. Paul puts the rapture and the day of the Lord after the revealing of the Antichrist.

Paul never taught that the next event on the prophetic calendar would be the rapture, as many Christians today believe. Paul would have talked about the rapture more than the Apostasy and the revealing of the man of sin.

Paul stressed that the believer would not be surprised at the coming of the day of the Lord. Only the unbeliever would be surprised.

Summary

The pre-tribulation rapture position stance is wrong.

Paul did not state that the rapture would begin before the revealing of the Antichrist. Paul intimately ties the rapture and the day of the Lord together. And the day of the Lord follows the revealing of the Antichrist. So the day of the Lord and the rapture occur sometime after the revealing of the man of lawlessness.

Paul also never stated that the revealing of the man of lawlessness is the beginning of the day of the Lord. Paul only states the day of the Lord will follow the revealing of the man of lawlessness.

The only revealing of the man of lawlessness that Paul mentions or describes is found in 2 Thess 2:4, and this states, "He will oppose and will exalt himself over everything that is called God or is worshiped, so that he sets himself up in God's temple, proclaiming himself to be God."

It is in 2 Thess 2:4 where the revealing of the Antichrist takes place. In the Thessalonian letters, Paul does not mention the signing of the covenant with many. Paul describes the abomination of desolation, not the start of Daniel's seventieth week.

The day of the Lord and the rapture follow the revealing of the Antichrist. The revealing of who and what the Antichrist does is at the abomination of desolation. The day of the Lord and the rapture follow the abomination of desolation.

The day of the Lord and the rapture do not take the believer by surprise. The believer is a son of the light. The believer will see the revealing of the Antichrist. The revealing of the Antichrist occurs before the day of the Lord.

The day of the Lord follows the revealing of the Antichrist. The day of the Lord does not take the believer by surprise. Since the day of the Lord does not happen until after the revealing of the man of lawlessness, the day of the Lord does not include Daniel's seventieth week.

CHAPTER 9

The Day of the Lord Follows the Apostasy

The pre-tribulation rapture position holds to an idea that after the rapture occurs, there will be a great revival. They believe that after the rapture, God will save and seal 144,000 Jews. They will be 144,000 born again Jewish believers in Jesus.

These 144,000 Jews will be 144,000 witnesses for Christ. They will carry the burden of preaching the good news to the entire world. They believe the vacuum of believers by the rapture of the church before the seventieth week of Daniel will be filled by these 144,000 evangelists.

Their belief is that the 144,000 witnesses will produce a great revival. Most of those who will have accepted Jesus through the preaching of the 144,000 will be martyred for their faith.

This train of thought is nothing more than a theory. The 144,000 sealed Jews are never mentioned as being born again, witnesses, or evangelists. The 144,000 sealed Jews are not mentioned as taking the gospel to the ends of the earth or being responsible for a revival during the seventieth week of Daniel.

The pre-tribulation rapture position idea of a revival comes from two passages of scriptures. It is from Acts 2:17-21 and Revelation 7:9-17. Given below is the Acts passage.

> In the last days, God says,
> I will pour out my Spirit on all people.
> Your sons and daughters will prophesy,
> your young men will see visions,

your old men will dream dreams.
Even on my servants, both men and women,
I will pour out my Spirit in those days,
and they will prophesy.
I will show wonders in the heaven above
and signs on the earth below,
blood and fire and billows of smoke.
The sun will be turned to darkness
and the moon to blood
before the coming of the great and glorious day of the Lord.
And everyone who calls
on the name of the Lord will be saved.

The very first of this passage, "In the last days," throws off a number of believers. Some see the term, "last days," and automatically associate the phrase with the seventieth week of Daniel. The "last days" here refer from the day of Pentecost to the second coming of Jesus. So far, the last days have lasted over nineteen hundred years.

In the last days, God will pour out his spirit on all people. Peter and the others were just filled with the Holy Spirit. They were speaking in tongues. People from every nation were in Jerusalem at that time. These Galileans were speaking in the languages of the foreigners. The people in the crowd asked each other what does this mean? Then Peter gave his famous sermon using the above text and others and about 3,000 people were saved!

The last days are still today and the function of the Holy Spirit is still the same. No spiritual gift is to be lacking as we wait for Jesus to be revealed (1 Cor 1: 7)-when the perfection comes (1 Cor 13: 10) and when the mortal puts on immortality (1 Cor 15:53). The great commission of Mark 16: 15-18 has the gifts of the spirit attributed to the believer. "And surely I am with you to the end of the age, "states Matthew 28:20.

Revelation 7:9-17 is also used by the pre-tribulation rapture position to support a great revival during the seventieth week of Daniel.

After this I looked and there before me was a great multitude that no one could count, from every nation, tribe, people and language, standing before the throne and in front of the Lamb. They were wearing white robes and were holding palm branches in their hands. And they cried out in a loud voice:

"Salvation belongs to our God,
who sits on the throne,
and to the Lamb."

All the angels were standing around the throne and around the elders
and the four living creatures. They fell down on their faces before the
throne and worshiped God, saying:

"Amen!
Praise and glory
and wisdom and thanks and honor
and power and strength
be to our God for ever and ever.
Amen!"

Then one of the elders asked me" "These in white robes-who are they,
and where did they come from?"

I answered, "Sir, you know."

And he said, "These are they who have come out of the great
tribulation; they have washed their robes and made them white in the
blood of the Lamb. Therefore,

"they are before the throne of God"
and serve him day and night in his temple;
and he who sits on the throne will spread his tent over them.
Never again will they hunger;
never again will they thirst.
The sun will not beat upon them,
nor any scorching heat.
For the Lamb at the center of the throne will be their shepherd;
he will lead them to springs of living water.
And God will wipe away every tear from their eyes."

The above scripture is used to support a revival in the last days. It
is taken by pre-tribulation rapture believers to be a revival, a great soul
harvest. They believe the 144,000 sealed Jews are 144,000 evangelists for

Christ.[13][14][15][16] The 144,000 Jews go into the world, proclaim the gospel, and see millions saved. Most of those new believers will be martyred during the great tribulation.[17] The pre-tribulation rapture believers suppose that since the church was taken up in the rapture before Daniel's seventieth week began, the 144,000 Jews were given the task of completing the great commission. The pre-tribulation rapture position believes the sealing of the 144,00 Jews takes place at the beginning of Daniel's seventieth week[18], and they also believe the great multitude of Rev 7:9-17 are martyred Christians who found their salvation during the last seven years of the time of the Gentiles.

After the sixth seal is broken, Rev 7:1 begins with the word "After" or "And after." The bible uses the Greek preposition "meta", and Strong's Numbers Reference defines "meta" as with, after, or behind. Most translations use the word "after" as the interpretation of the word "meta."

The sealing of the 144,000 Jews is after the sixth seal but before the rapture of the saints (the great multitude of Rev 7:7-19) and the opening of the seventh seal.

Never are the 144,000 Jews mentioned as witnesses. Nowhere in the Bible are they called evangelists, as has been popularly proclaimed.[19] We do know that 12,000 Jews from twelve of the tribes of Israel are sealed. Also in chapter fourteen of Revelation, we find they did not defile themselves with women, for they kept themselves pure. To call the 144,000 sealed Jews evangelists is just an assumption.

The great multitude of Rev 7:9 is described with the same words found in Rev 5:9-10-every tribe and language and people and nation. These are people bought with the blood of Jesus for God the Father (Rev5: 9).

---

13   Hal Lindsey, The Rapture(New York: Bantam Books,1983),173

14   Tim Lahaye, The Rapture(Oregon: Harvest House Publishing,2002),131

15   Mark Hitchcock and Thomas Ice, The Truth Behind Left Behind (Oregon: Multnomah Publishers, 2004),83

16   J. Dwight Pentecost, Prophecy for Today(Michigan: Discovery House Publishers, 1989),47

17   Mark Hitchcock and Thomas Ice, The Truth Behind Left Behind (Oregon: Multnomah Publishers, 2004),77

18   Hal Lindsey, The Rapture(New York: Bantam Books,1983),8

19   Marvin Rosenthal, The Pre-wrath Rapture of the Church(Tennessee: Thomas Nelson Inc., 1990),182

The great multitude is raptured saints; not martyred believers. A martyred group of souls was found in the opening of the fifth seal. So the question begs, why would we see another group of martyrs between the sixth and seventh seals?

Some of the confusion comes when one of the elders answered John in Rev 7:14 about the identity of the great multitude. The elder stated, "These are they who have come out of the great tribulation; they have washed their robes in the blood of the Lamb." Some people have believed this to have meant martyrdom for the Christian. But, washed their robes in the blood of the Lamb does not mean they died for Christ (martyrs) as popularized by some pre-tribulation authors. These are people who have washed their sin away in the blood of Jesus. References for the washing away our sins can be found in 1 Cor 6:11, Eph 5:26, Titus 3:5, Rev 22:14, Acts 22:16, Psalm 51:7, Hebrews 10:22, and the great hymn "Are You Washed in the Blood." These are born again believers in Jesus.

Pre-tribulation rapture believers hold to the great multitude standing before the throne and the Lamb as martyred saints from the resultant work of 144,000 sealed Jewish witnesses for Christ. Revelation chapter seven does not state either one of these theories. Nowhere in scripture does it say that the 144,000 Jews are witnessing for Christ. Nowhere in chapter seven of revelation does it say the great multitude have been murdered or given their physical life for the sake of the cross.

The outpouring of the Holy Spirit shall last until the end of the age, but the end of the age shall be filled with apostasy.

Scriptural Support of the Apostasy

1. The Laodicean church is the last church in the succession of seven if you hold to believing the seven churches of Rev 2-3 are representative of the church throughout its' history. The Laodicean church is a dead church. Given is the suppositional dating of the church from the book of Revelation:

1. Ephesus–The Apostolic Church 30-100-.D.
2. Smryna–The Persecuted Church 100-313 A.D.
3. Pergamos-The State Church 313-590 A.D.
4. Thyatira–The Papal Church 590-1517 A.D.
5. Sardis–The Reformed Church 1517-1790 A.D.
6. Philadelphia–The Missionary Church 1790-1900 A.D.

7 Laodicea–The Apostate Church 1900-present[20]

The Laodicean church is a dead church.

2. 2 Thes 2:3 states the day of the Lord will not come until the rebellion occurs and the man of lawlessness is revealed. The word "rebellion" is translated from the Greek word "apostia." Apostia means a falling away, defection, and apostasy.

3. Matt 24:4-5, Mark 13:5-6, and Luke 21:8 warn about false christs and that many will be deceived. This may correspond to the opening of the first seal. (Rev 6:1-2)

4. Going along with number three. Matt 24:9-13 and Mark 13:12-13 state that wickedness and the love of most will grow cold. There will be a turning away from the faith. Children will rebel against the parents and have them killed. Brother against brother and a father against his child.

5. 1 Tim 4:1-5 in latter times some will abandon the faith and follow deceiving spirits. They forbid people to marry and order them to abstain from certain foods.

6. 2 Tim 3:1-5 This is the famous and often quoted passage that starts with, "But mark this: There will be terrible times in the last days," and then Paul goes on to give the list-lovers of themselves, lovers of money, boastful, proud, abusive, disobedient to parents, ungrateful, unholy, without love, unforgiving, slanderous, without self-control, brutal, not lovers of the good, treacherous, rash, conceited, lovers of pleasure rather than lovers of God-having a form of godliness but denying it's power-so professing Christ but not really a heart for Christ. Again, is it the Laodicean church?

Apostasy will reign at the end of the age, not revival. Persecution of both the Jew and the Christian will occur in Daniel's seventieth week.

In Revelation chapter twelve, Satan is cast out of heaven and has three and a half years left before he will be bound in the abyss for a thousand years. (Rev 20:1-3) This will probably take place around the midway point of Daniel's seventieth week. Somewhere around this point according to Matt 24:15-20, Mark 13:14-17, and Daniel 9:27, the antichrist will set up an abomination that causes desolation in the new temple in Jerusalem. After Satan is cast out of heaven, he goes after God's chosen people-the Jews, but God will prepare a place for the Jews for 1,260 days, three and

---

20   Marvin Rosenthal, The Pre-wrath Rapture of the Church(Tennessee: Thomas Nelson Inc., 1990),287

a half years, forty-two months, or otherwise phrased time, times, and half a time—a time being equal to a year. Satan is upset at the escape of Israel so he goes off to make war against those who hold to the testimony of Jesus.

Satan gives his authority to the beast (antichrist, little horn). (Rev13: 4) The beast is allowed to exercise his authority for forty-two months. He blasphemes God—his name, dwelling place, and those who live in heaven. The antichrist was given authority over every tribe, people, language, and nation. He was given power to make war against the saints and to conquer them. (Rev 13:5-8) Antichrist will imprison and kill the saints. Satan declares one last major surge against the Jews and believers in Christ.

Saints in the Old Testament refer to believers in the God of Israel. Saints in the New Testament are the true believers in Jesus (those who are washed in the blood).

Daniel 7:21-22 also sees the beast waging war against the saints and defeating them until the time Jesus comes and sets up his kingdom on earth. Daniel 7:25 also states the saints will be handed over to the antichrist for three and a half years.

Summary

There will not be revival in the very last of days. It will be filled with a turning away from faith in Jesus. There will be persecution unto death for both the Jew and the Christian. The love of most will grow cold.

The Apostle Paul states that the apostasy will occur before the day of the Lord. The day of the Lord and the rapture are intimately tied together. The rapture follows the apostasy.

The rapture comes at the end of the seventieth week of Daniel (post-tribulation), not before the seventieth week of Daniel (pre-tribulation).

CHAPTER 10

The Day of the Lord will not take the Believer by Surprise

But the day of the Lord will come like a thief.—2 Peter 3:10

"Behold, I come like a thief! Blessed is he who stays awake and keeps his clothes with him, so that he may not go naked and be shamefully exposed."-Revelation 16:15

Remember, therefore, what you have received and heard; obey it, and repent. But if you do not wake up, I will come like a thief, and you will not know at what time I will come to you.-Revelation 3:3

Therefore keep watch, because you do not know on what day your Lord will come. But understand this: If the owner of the house had known at what time of night the thief was coming, he would have kept watch and would not have let his house be broken into. So you also must be ready, because the Son of Man will come at an hour when you do not expect him.—Matthew 24:42-44

The pre-tribulation rapture position believes in Jesus coming once for the rapture of the church. Then Jesus comes back a second time seven plus years to reign on the earth. It is their belief that Jesus will come like a thief in the night. Both the saved and the unsaved will be caught off guard at the rapture of the church.

But the saved Christian will have a general idea about the timing of the second coming of Jesus despite what the pre-tribulation rapture position believes. Of course we do not know which exact day or the time of Jesus' arrival might be. But we do know there are four signs that come before the day of the Lord/rapture (cosmic disturbance, an Elijah, the revealing of the Antichrist, and the apostasy). The day of the Lord/rapture will not take the believer by surprise.

Now, brothers, about times and dates we do not need to write to *you*, for *you* know very well that the day of the Lord will come like a thief in the night. While *people* are saying, "Peace and safety," destruction will come on *them* suddenly, as labor pains on a pregnant woman, and *they* will not escape. But *you*, brothers, are not in darkness so that this day should surprise *you* like a thief. *You* are all sons of the light and sons of the day. *We* do not belong to the night or to the darkness. So then, let *us* not be like *others*, who are asleep, but let *us* be alert and self-controlled. For *those* who sleep, sleep at night, and *those* who get drunk, get drunk at night. But since *we* belong to the day, let *us* be self-controlled, putting on faith and love as a breastplate, and the hope of salvation as a helmet. For God did not appoint *us* to suffer wrath but to receive salvation through *our* Lord Jesus Christ. He died for *us* so that, whether *we* are awake or asleep, *we* may live together with him. Therefore encourage one another and build each other up, just as in fact *you* are doing. (1 Thessalonians 5:1-11) (Italics mine)

First, the reader will have to reread these verses (1 Thessalonians 5:1-11) focusing on the pronouns and nouns such as people, you, them, they, we and us. Paul speaks of two different groups of people. Paul speaks of the saved (Christian) and the unsaved (non-Christian). The unsaved will be surprised at the day of the Lord. The saved will not be surprised at the day of the Lord.

The people who belong to the darkness (the unsaved) will be saying, "Peace and safety," but then the sudden destruction associated with the day of the Lord will take them by surprise.

But the brethren who are the sons of the day (the saved) should not be surprised when this day comes (1 Thess 5:4). The children of God are to be self-controlled and alert. Their feet are to be fitted with the readiness that comes from the gospel of peace, with the buckle of truth around the waist; with the breastplate of love and righteousness in place; they are to take up the shield of faith to extinguish all the flaming arrows of the evil one; the hope of salvation as a helmet, and the sword of the Spirit (the word of God). We are to be ready for Christ.

1 Thess 5:9-10 states, "For God did not appoint us to suffer wrath," Some pre-tribulation rapture believers stop the verses right here. They use those words to say that the rapture will keep them from the wrath of

God and the wrath of God includes the entire seventieth week of Daniel. This partial verse does not support a pre-tribulation rapture before the beginning of Daniel's seventieth week. They leave out the rest of verse nine and verse ten.

Again, 1 Thess 5:9-10 states, "For God did not appoint us to suffer wrath, but to receive salvation through our Lord Jesus Christ. He died for us so that whether we are awake or asleep, we may live together with him." If we have died in Christ, you shall not suffer wrath from God (the lake of burning fire). If we are awake (alive), we shall not suffer the wrath of God in the day of the Lord. The believer who has the hope of salvation and the shield of faith will be raptured at the start of the day of the Lord. And the day of the Lord does not occur until after the cosmic disturbance, an Elijah, the revealing of the man of lawlessness, and the apostasy.

1 Thess 5:1-11 and 2 Thess 2:1-2 states that the day of the Lord is associated with the rapture. And the believer should have an idea of the general time of when the day of the Lord and the rapture should take place. That day should not overtake the believer like a thief in the night. Only the unbeliever should be surprised.

In Matthew 24:32-35, Mark 13:28-31, and Luke 21:28-33, Jesus tells us the parable of the fig tree. As soon as the twigs get tender and the leaves come out, you know that summer is near. The generation who is alive and see the events (cosmic disturbance, an Elijah, the revealing of the man of lawlessness, and the apostasy) occurring shall not pass away. Luke adds when these things begin to take place, stand up and lift up your heads, because your redemption is drawing near.

Luke exhorts us to watch and pray that we may be able to escape all that is about to happen. (Luke 21:36)

Summary

The day of the Lord will overtake the unbeliever like a thief in the night.

The believer shall be watching and not be taken by surprise when the day of the Lord comes.

CHAPTER 11

The Lord Alone will be Exalted in that Day, Not the Antichrist

The eyes of the arrogant man will be humbled and the pride of men brought low; the LORD alone will be exalted in that day. (Isaiah 2:11)

The arrogance of man will be brought low and the pride of men humbled; the LORD alone will be exalted in that day, and the idols will totally disappear.(Isaiah 2:17)

It is the Lord, and the Lord alone who will be exalted during the day of the Lord.

The seventieth week of Daniel is presumed to part of the day of the Lord by the pre-tribulation rapture position. In Isaiah 2:11, 17, 18 it is stated in that day, the Lord alone will be exalted. The "day," Isaiah is referring to is the day of the Lord.

During the seventieth week of Daniel, the Antichrist will be exalted and worshipped on the earth. So if the Antichrist is exalted during the seventieth week of Daniel, the seventieth week of Daniel cannot be part of the day of the Lord.

During the day of the Lord, the Lord alone will be exalted.

The last half of Daniel's seventieth week is the reign of the Antichrist.

Satan has three and a half years to bring hell on Earth before his one thousand year sentence commences. Satan's anger is turned towards the believers in Christ.

Satan gives his authority to the beast or otherwise known as the Antichrist or the man of lawlessness. (Rev 13:4)

The Antichrist exercises his authority for forty-two months. (Rev 13:5)

The Antichrist blasphemes God, slanders his name, his dwelling place, and those who live in heaven. (Rev 13:6)

The Antichrist will try to change the set times and laws. (Daniel 7:25)

The Antichrist will oppress the saints, and the saints will be handed to Antichrist for three and a half years. Antichrist will make war against the saints. (Rev 13:7 & Daniel 7:25-26)

The Antichrist will be given authority over every tribe, people, language, and nation. (Rev 13:7)

The Antichrist will be worshipped by everyone except those whose names are written in the book of life. (Rev 13:8)

The Antichrist will commit the abomination of desolation. (Daniel 9:27, Matthew 24:15, and Mark 13:14)

The Antichrist will proclaim himself to be called God. (2 Thess 2:4)

Those who refuse to worship the image of the beast shall be killed. (Rev 3:15)

The Antichrist will also force everyone to receive a mark on his right hand or forehead. No one will be able to buy or sell without the mark of the beast. (Rev 13:16-17)

The beast (Antichrist) rules during the last half of Daniel's seventieth week. The Antichrist proclaims himself to be God. He calls the world to worship him. They show obedience to the Antichrist by receiving the mark. The saints will refuse. The saints will be handed to the Antichrist. He will make war against the saints and try to kill them.

But according to the prophet Isaiah, the Lord alone will be exalted in that day. Therefore, the seventieth week of Daniel cannot be part of the day of the Lord because the Antichrist is exalted during the seventieth week of Daniel.

Summary

The Lord alone will be exalted in that day. (Isaiah 2:11)

The eyes of the arrogant man will be humbled and the pride of men brought low; the LORD alone will be exalted in that day. (Isaiah 2:11)

The Antichrist will be worshipped during the last half of Daniel's seventieth week. The Antichrist will rule the world during the last half of Daniel's seventieth week. Since the Lord alone will be exalted during the day of the Lord, no part of Daniel's seventieth week can be called the day of the Lord.

The day of the Lord cannot be part of Daniel's seventieth week. For the Lord alone will be exalted on the day of the Lord. It is called the *day* of the Lord.

CHAPTER 12

The Olivet Discourse Ties it Together Chronologically

Jesus had left the Jewish temple and made his way up to the Mount of Olives. On the Mount of Olives, Jesus' disciples ask him two questions. Jesus gave a lengthy discourse (talk or conversation) on the two questions asked of him. Hence this is how we get the term, "The Olivet Discourse."

Jesus had said these words as they were leaving the temple. "Do you see all these things? I tell you the truth, not one stone here will be left on another; everyone will be thrown down."

The first question from the disciples was when this will happen.

Jesus responded with the following

"Watch out that no one deceives you. For many will come in my name, claiming, 'I am the Messiah,' and will deceive many. You will hear of wars and rumors of wars, but see to it that you are not alarmed. Such things must happen, but the end is still to come. Nation will rise against nation, and kingdom against kingdom. There will be famines and earthquakes in various places. All these are the beginning of birth pains.

"Then you will be handed over to be persecuted and put to death, and you will be hated by all nations because of me. At that time many will turn away from the faith and will betray and hate each other, and many false prophets will appear and deceive many people. Because of the increase of wickedness, the love of most will grow cold, but the one who stands firm to the end will be saved. And this gospel of the kingdom will be preached in the whole world as a testimony to all nations, and then the end will come." (Matt 24:4-14)

The disciples were to endure persecution for their faith in Jesus. Some of them were to be put to death. The disciples were to be hated by most people. This all came true as Jesus said it would.

False prophets appeared in the apostolic age. John in his letters warned his beloved to be on their guard against the spirit of falsehood. And Paul in his letter to the Galatians warned them about people trying to pervert the gospel of Jesus.

These events that Jesus foretold occurred and then in 70 A.D. the temple of Jerusalem was totally destroyed by the Roman army under General Titus. Jesus had answered the first question about when the destruction of the temple would take place. He did not give a specific date or year. He had given the disciples signs that would take place before the fulfillment.

This was how Jesus answered the second question posed by the disciples. "What will be the sign of your coming and of the end of the age?"

The preceding verses (Matt 24:4-14) may have a double implication. The above verses could correspond to the events of 70 A.D. and earlier, but they may also be included as signs to the very last of days. Evidence for this theory is in verse 14 (And this gospel of the kingdom will be preached in the whole world as a testimony to all nations, and then the end will come.)

In Matt 24: 15-20, the abomination of desolation takes place. This corresponds to the revealing of the man of lawlessness spoken of by the apostle Paul in 2 Thess 2:1-4. The desecration of the temple occurs around the middle of the seventieth week of Daniel. (Daniel 9:27)

A glimpse into the second half of the week of Daniel is given in Matt 24:21-28. The distresses

"So when you see standing in the holy place 'the abomination that causes desolation,' spoken of through the prophet Daniel—let the reader understand—then let those who are in Judea flee to the mountains. Let no one on the housetop go down to take anything out of the house. Let no one in the field go back to get their cloak. How dreadful it will be in those days for pregnant women and nursing mothers! Pray that your flight will not take place in winter or on the Sabbath."
(Matt 24:15-20)

of those days are never to be equaled again! In this section, there is the repeated warning about false prophets and now also false christs. There is going to be deception of some kind to try to deceive the elect. Paul also states this in 2 Thess 2:9-12. In 2 Thess 2:9, the coming of the lawless one will be with false miracles, wonders, and different types of deceptions. God will send a delusion so that they will believe the lie.

The elect (Christian) are encouraged not to believe in the false prophets or their deceptions. The coming of Jesus will be visible to everyone. There will be no doubt when Jesus appears. The world will know.

> "For then there will be great distress, unequaled from the beginning of the world until now—and never to be equaled again.
>
> If those days had not been cut short, no one would survive, but for the sake of the elect those days will be shortened. At that time if anyone says to you, 'Look, here is the Messiah!' or, 'There he is!' do not believe it. For false messiahs and false prophets will appear and perform great signs and wonders to deceive, if possible, even the elect. See, I have told you ahead of time.
>
> So if anyone tells you, 'There he is, out in the wilderness,' do not go out; or, 'Here he is, in the inner rooms,' do not believe it. For as lightning that comes from the east is visible even in the west, so will be the coming of the Son of Man. Wherever there is a carcass, there the vultures will gather."(Matt 24:21-28)

The cosmic disturbance takes place in Matt24:29
(Immediately after the distress of those days
the sun will be darkened,
and the moon will not give its light;
the stars will fall from the sky,
and the heavenly bodies will be shaken.)
Jesus appears.
Matt 24:30 (Then will appear the sign of the Son of Man in heaven. And then all the peoples of the earth will mourn when they see the Son of Man coming on the clouds of heaven, with power and great glory)

The world will see Jesus. The sign of the Son of Man will appear. The disciple's second question was answered. (What will be the sign of your coming and of the end of the age?") The cosmic disturbance, the apostasy, and the abomination of desolation were all referenced by Jesus to happen before his coming.

Matt 24:31 (And he will send his angels with a loud trumpet call, and they will gather his elect from the four winds, from one end of the heavens to the other.)

The rapture event takes place.

According to Jesus, the falling away (the apostasy), the abomination of desolation (the revealing of the man of lawlessness), and the cosmic disturbance takes place before the rapture.

The pre-tribulation rapture is false. The pre-tribulation rapture does not match up with the words of Jesus.

The rapture is a post-tribulation rapture occurring after the signs mentioned above. The rapture takes place at the end of the seventieth week of Daniel.

Summary

Jesus in his Olivet Discourse clearly shows a rise in wickedness, the love of many growing cold, and a falling away (apostasy) occurring before his second coming.

Jesus also puts the abomination of desolation before his second coming.

Jesus states the cosmic disturbance takes place before his second coming.

Jesus appears to the world after these signs take place.

The rapture event takes place at his appearing.

The Olivet Discourse gives a chronological sequence of events leading up to the day of the Lord/rapture (second coming of Jesus). We must take the King of kings at his word!

CHAPTER 13

Imminence?

According to the pre-tribulation rapture position, the rapture is an imminent event, and no other signs or events need to take place before the rapture will happen.

This chapter will look at the verses in which the pre-tribulation rapture position claims to show evidence that the rapture is an imminent event.

By the end of this chapter, it will be clear that there are no verses supporting the idea of an imminent return of Jesus.

(John 14:1-3, Do not let your hearts be troubled. Trust in God; trust also in me. In my Father's house are many rooms; if it were not so, I would have told you. I am going there to prepare a place for you. And if I go and prepare a place for you, I will come back and take you to be with me that you also may be where I am.)[21]

Jesus is preparing a place for us. Jesus will come again and receive us to himself. We will be together with the Lord.

What John 14:1-3 does not say is when the rapture will occur or if the rapture could happen at any time.

(1 John 3:1-3, how great is the love the Father has lavished on us, that we should be called children of God! And that is what we are! The reason the world does not know us is that it did not know him. Dear friends, now we are children of God, and what we will be has not yet been made

---

21   John Walvoord, The Rapture Question(Grand Rapids: Zondervan Publishing House,1979),70

known. But we know that when he appears, we shall be like him, for we shall see him as he is. Everyone who has this hope in him purifies himself, just as he is pure.)[22]

We are God's children, but what we will be like in our future body is not yet known. When Jesus appears (or is revealed) at the rapture, we who are alive or dead shall have our mortal bodies changed to immortal bodies. Paul writes about the perishable body transforming to the imperishable body in 1 Corinthians 15:51-53.

Therefore, when Jesus appears our bodies shall be transformed and we shall be with the Lord forever.

What John 3:1-3 does not say is when the rapture will occur or if the rapture could happen at any time.

1 Thessalonians chapters four and five are stated as contributing to theory of imminence.[23] More specifically 1 Thessalonians 4:13 through 5:11 talk about the rapture and it's connection to the day of the Lord. These scriptures shall be separated into 1 Thess 4:13-18 and the 1 Thess 5:1-11.

(1 Thessalonians 4:13-18, Brothers, we do not want you to be ignorant about those who fall asleep, or to grieve like the rest of men, who have no hope. We believe that Jesus died and rose again and so we believe that God will bring with Jesus those who have fallen asleep in him. According to the Lord's own word, we tell you that we who are still alive, who are left till the coming of the Lord, will certainly not precede those who have fallen asleep. For the Lord himself will come down from heaven, with a loud command, with the voice of the archangel and with the trumpet call of God, and the dead in Christ will rise first. After that, we who are still alive and are left will be caught up together with them in the clouds to meet the Lord in the air. And so we will be with the Lord forever. Therefore encourage each other with these words.)—"The Rapture Passage"

There will be a loud command.
With the voice of the archangel.
With the trumpet call of God.
The dead in Christ will rise first.

---

22   John Walvoord, The Rapture Question(Grand Rapids: Zondervan Publishing House,1979),70

23   John Walvoord, The Rapture Question(Grand Rapids: Zondervan Publishing House,1979),70

After that, the saints who are alive and left will be raptured to meet the Lord in the clouds. The saints will now be with the Lord forever; encourage each other with these words.

What 1 Thess 4:13-18 does not say is when the rapture will occur or if the rapture could happen at any time.

(1 Thessalonians 5:1-11, Now, brothers, about times and dates *we* do not need to write to *you*, for *you* know very well that the day of the Lord will come like a thief in the night. While people are saying, "Peace and safety," destruction will come on them suddenly, as labor pains on a pregnant woman, and they will not escape.

But *you*, brothers, are not in darkness so that this day should surprise *you* like a thief. *You* are all sons of the light and sons of the day. *We* do not belong to the night or to the darkness. So then, let *us* not be like others, who are asleep, but let *us* be alert and self-controlled. For those who sleep, sleep at night, and those who get drunk, get drunk at night. But since *we* belong to the day, let *us* be self-controlled, putting on faith and love as a breastplate, and the hope of salvation as a helmet. For God did not appoint *us* to suffer wrath but to receive salvation through our Lord Jesus Christ. He died for *us* so that, whether *we* are awake or asleep, *we* may live together with him. Therefore encourage one another and build each other up, just as in fact *you* are doing) The underlining and the italics are used to show that Paul was talking about two different groups of people. They were the saved and the unsaved.

The day of the Lord should not overtake the believer like a thief in the night. Only the unbeliever should be surprised.

What 1 Thess 5:1-11 does not state is that the rapture is an imminent event. Quite the opposite when 2 Thessalonians 2:1-4 is read.

(2 Thessalonians 2:1-4, Concerning the coming of our Lord Jesus Christ and our being gathered to him, we ask you, brothers, not to become easily unsettled or alarmed by some prophecy, report, or letter supposed to have come from us, saying that the day of the Lord has already come. Don't let anyone deceive you in any way, for that day will not come until the rebellion occurs and the man of lawlessness is revealed, the man doomed to destruction. He will oppose and will exalt himself over everything that is called God or is worshiped, so that he sets himself up in God's temple, proclaiming himself to be God.)

The rapture (our being gathered to him) and the day of the Lord are linked together in this verse by Paul. The day of the Lord/rapture follows the apostasy and the revealing of the man of lawlessness.

The rapture cannot come before the apostasy and the revealing of the man of lawlessness. That would be against the word of God. The rapture cannot be imminent.

(1 Cor 1:7, Therefore you do not lack any spiritual gift as you eagerly wait for our Lord Jesus Christ to be revealed.)

Awaiting eagerly the revelation (coming in the KJV) of our Lord Jesus Christ. Jesus is going to be revealed. The word revealed is from the Greek word "*apokalupis*" which means an unveiling or revelation. This word emphasizes the visibility of the Lord's return. It is used of the Lord (2Thess 1:7, 1Pet 1:7, 13, 4:13), of the sons of God in connection with the Lord's return (Rom 8:19) and of the man of lawlessness (2 Thess 2:6, 8), and always implies perceptibility.[24]

The church is not to lack any spiritual gift as it waits the revealing of our Lord Jesus Christ. When Jesus appears we shall be like him. The perfection will come. The mortal will put on immortality.

What the scripture is saying is that Jesus will be seen. Some pre-tribulation authors use 1Cor 1:7 for imminence.[25] The pre-tribulation rapture position believes in rapture where none of those left on the earth after a pre-tribulation rapture will have seen Jesus. The people of the world left behind would not have seen Jesus calling his bride home. In this verse Jesus is revealed.

This verse is presenting scriptural support for the post-tribulation rapture position by the verse stating Jesus will be seen at the rapture. (If you want to call this verse a rapture passage.)

What 1 Cor 1:7 does not say is when the rapture will occur or if it could happen at any time. The scripture states that we are not to lack any spiritual gift as we wait for the Lord Jesus Christ to be revealed.

---

24   Oxford NIV Scofield Study Bible (1984 edition),1197
25   Mark Hitchcock and Thomas Ice, The Truth Behind Left Behind (Oregon: Multnomah Publishers, 2004),39

Cor 16:22, If anyone does not love the Lord—a curse be on him. Come, O Lord!) They key in the word "maranatha."[26]

In the NIV, maranatha is translated, "Come, O Lord!".

Some other translations of the Greek word "maranatha" include, "The Lord is coming soon," or "our Lord cometh."

What 1 Cor 16:22 does not say is when the rapture will occur or if it could happen at any time.

(Phil 3:20) It would be helpful to add verse 21 to this passage. (Phil 3:20-21, But our citizenship is in heaven. And we eagerly await a Savior from there, the Lord Jesus Christ, who, by the power that enables him to bring everything under his control, will transform our lowly bodies so that they will be like his glorious body.)[27]

It is with great anticipation that the believers look forward to the second coming of Jesus. For when Jesus comes, he shall transform our mortal bodies into immortal bodies. The time, in which Jesus transforms our lowly bodies, so that they will be like his, is at the rapture.

What Phil 3:20-21 does not say is when the rapture will occur or if it could happen at any time.

(Phil 4:5, Let your gentleness be evident to all. The Lord is near.)

They key in on the phrase, "The Lord is near." [28] With a reading of chapter four completely, a conclusion can be drawn that this phrase is not eschatological. Even if the term is eschatological, it is fine. Ever since Jesus ascended to heaven, we have been living in the last days. (Acts 2:17-21, Joel 2:28-32, I Pet 4:7, 1 John 2:18, and James 5:8)

What Phil 4:5 does not say is when the rapture will occur or if it could happen at any time.

(1 Thess 1:10, and to wait for his Son from heaven, whom he raised from the dead—Jesus, who rescues us from the coming wrath.)

---

[26] Mark Hitchcock and Thomas Ice, The Truth Behind Left Behind (Oregon: Multnomah Publishers, 2004),39

[27] Mark Hitchcock and Thomas Ice, The Truth Behind Left Behind (Oregon: Multnomah Publishers, 2004),39

[28] Mark Hitchcock and Thomas Ice, The Truth Behind Left Behind (Oregon: Multnomah Publishers, 2004),39

We are told to wait for Jesus who will rescue us from the coming wrath. Jesus will rapture us before the day of the Lord comes. Isaiah 13:9, "See, the day of the Lord is coming-a cruel day, with wrath and fierce anger-to make the land desolate and destroy the sinners within it." The wrath of God is associated with day of the Lord, and the day of the Lord comes after the cosmic disturbance (The sun will be turned to darkness and the moon to blood before the coming of the great and dreadful day of the Lord. Joel 2:30 and Acts 2:20). Jesus will remove his bride from the earth before he makes man scarcer than pure gold. "Alas for that day! For the day of the Lord is near; it will come like destruction from the Almighty." (Joel 1:15)

What 1 Thess 1:10 does not say is when the rapture will occur or if it could happen at any time.

(Titus 2:13) The inclusion of verses 11-14 would be helpful. (Titus 2:11-14, For the grace of God that brings salvation has appeared to all men. It teaches us to say "No" to ungodliness and worldly passions, and to live self-controlled, upright and godly lives in this present age, while we wait for the blessed hope—the glorious appearing of our great God and Savior, Jesus Christ, who gave himself for us to redeem us from all wickedness and to purify for himself a people that are his very own, eager to do what is good.)[29]

Jesus is the blessed hope and his glorious appearing will take us home to be with him forever.

Some pre-tribulation rapture authors hold to the "blessed hope" of Titus 2:13 being synonymous with the rapture. Tim LaHaye wrote, "Paul's "Blessed hope" is the Rapture."[30] Mark Hitchcock and Thomas Ice also refer to the rapture as the blessed hope.[31] There is no scriptural support for calling the blessed hope the rapture. Jesus is our blessed hope.

What Titus 2:13 does not say is when the rapture will occur or if it could happen at any time.

---

[29] Mark Hitchcock and Thomas Ice, The Truth Behind Left Behind (Oregon: Multnomah Publishers, 2004),40

[30] Tim Lahaye, The Rapture(Oregon: Harvest House Publishing,2002),71

[31] Mark Hitchcock and Thomas Ice, The Truth Behind Left Behind (Oregon: Multnomah Publishers, 2004),41

(Heb 9:28, so Christ was sacrificed once to take away the sins of many people; and he will appear a second time, not to bear sin, but to bring salvation to those who are waiting for him.)[32]

Christ's first advent was the precious sacrifice of his sinless life. He will appear a second time to bring salvation to those who are waiting (looking in the KJV) for him. Jesus came once. He is going to come back a second time. He will make a second appearance on earth. This verse, like 1 Cor 1:7, is damaging to the pre-tribulation rapture position. In their position, Christ came the first time, he will come in the clouds and rapture the church, and he will come a third time to set up his kingdom. (There is a seven plus year interval between the rapture, and the millennial kingdom.) According to the pre-tribulation rapture position, when the rapture occurs no one will see Jesus, but the use of this verse (he will appear a second time) causes harm to its position.

What Heb 9:28 does not say is when the rapture will occur or if it could happen at any time.

(James 5:7-9, Be patient, then, brothers, until the Lord's coming. See how the farmer waits for the land to yield its valuable crop and how patient he is for the autumn and spring rains. You too, be patient and stand firm, because the Lord's coming is near. Don't grumble against each other, brothers, or you will be judged. The Judge is standing at the door!)[33]

Yes, the Lord is near, and the Judge (Jesus) is standing at the door, but we must be patient. For over 1800 years, Israel was not a nation and the rebuilding of the temple was a very remote possibility. Even during those times, God could have set in motion the events and culmination of the seventieth week of Daniel. God will bring about in his own time the appearing of our Lord Jesus Christ.

What James 5:7-9 does not say is when the rapture will occur or if it could happen at any time.

---

[32] Mark Hitchcock and Thomas Ice, The Truth Behind Left Behind (Oregon: Multnomah Publishers, 2004),40

[33] Mark Hitchcock and Thomas Ice, The Truth Behind Left Behind (Oregon: Multnomah Publishers, 2004),40

Pet 1:13, Therefore, prepare your minds for action; be self-controlled; set your hope fully on the grace to be given you when Jesus Christ is revealed.)[34]

When Jesus is revealed, we will really learn the wonderful grace Jesus has and will bestow on us.

What 1 Pet 1:13 does not say is when the rapture will occur or if it could happen at any time.

(Jude 21, Keep yourselves in God's love as you wait for the mercy of our Lord Jesus Christ to bring you to eternal life.)[35]

It is Jesus Christ who will bring us to eternal life. The mortal will be changed to immortal. (See 1 Cor 15:51-53)

What Jude 21 does not say is when the rapture will occur or if it could happen at any time.

(Rev 3:11, I am coming soon. Hold on to what you have, so that no one will take your crown.)

(Rev 22:7, "Behold, I am coming soon! Blessed is he who keeps the words of the prophecy in this book.")

(Rev 22:12, "Behold, I am coming soon! My reward is with me, and I will give to everyone according to what he has done.)

(Rev 22:20, He who testifies to these things says, "Yes, I am coming soon." Amen. Come, Lord Jesus.)[36]

"I am coming quickly." Amen. Come Lord Jesus. We are to look forward to the coming of Jesus.

What Rev 3:11, 22:7, 12, 20 does not say is when the rapture will occur or if it could happen at any time.

(Rev 3:10) The "ek" controversy. The whole letter to the church in Philadelphia should be read. (Rev 3:7-13, These are the words of him who is holy and true, who holds the key of David. What he opens no one can shut, and what he shuts no one can open. I know your deeds. See, I have

---

34   Mark Hitchcock and Thomas Ice, The Truth Behind Left Behind (Oregon: Multnomah Publishers, 2004),40

35   Mark Hitchcock and Thomas Ice, The Truth Behind Left Behind (Oregon: Multnomah Publishers, 2004),40

36   Mark Hitchcock and Thomas Ice, The Truth Behind Left Behind (Oregon: Multnomah Publishers, 2004),40

placed before you an open door that no one can shut. I know that you have little strength, yet you have kept my word and have not denied my name. I will make those who are of the synagogue of Satan, who claim to be Jews though they are not, but are liars—I will make them come and fall down at your feet and acknowledge that I have loved you. Since you have kept my command to endure patiently, *I will also keep you from the hour of trial that is going to come upon the whole world to test those who live on the earth.* I am coming soon. Hold on to what you have, so that no one will take your crown. Him who overcomes I will make a pillar in the temple of my God. Never again will he leave it. I will write on him the name of my God and the name of the city of my God, the new Jerusalem, which is coming down out of heaven from my God; and I will also write on him my new name. He who has an ear, let him hear what the Spirit says to the churches.) (Italics mine to emphasize Rev 3:10)

"Ek" is a Greek word, which we translate into the English word "from." Our verse, "I will keep you from the hour of trial that is going to come upon the whole world to test those who live on the earth."

The word "ek" (from) can be defined two ways in this verse:

1. Kept out of the trial or
2. Kept safe within the trial.

Your definition of the word "ek" helps determine your rapture position. There is no conclusive evidence whether you are "kept out of" or "kept safe from within."

Most books on the rapture do deal with this verse in length. Whatever positions the books have taken as their thesis, the author will come to the conclusion that Rev 3:10's "ek" supports their theory.

But what is the hour of trial that Rev 3:10 wants to keep the church of Philadelphia from?

Is the hour of trial a seven-year period?

The only seven-year period mentioned dealing with the end times is the seventieth week of Daniel. (Dan 9:24-27) All time periods mentioned in the book of Revelation cover a three and a half year period, and they are described in three different ways.

1. 42 months–(Rev 11:3, 13:5)
2. Time, times, and half a time–(Dan 12:7)

3. 1,260 days–(Rev 12:6)

Could the hour of trial be the one hour when the ten horns (who are the ten kings) receive authority as kings along with the beast? The ten kings and the beast will make war against the Lamb. Jesus (the King of kings and Lord of lords) will overcome them at final battle-the battle of Armageddon. Coming with Jesus, are the saints his called, chosen and faithful followers. (Rev 17:12-14)

At this point in history, what the hour of trial is and how long it lasts, is left to speculation and assumptions.

What Rev 3:10 does not say is when the rapture will occur or if it could happen at any time. It promises to keep a certain people from an hour of trial to come. What the hour of trial is usually depends on your rapture stance. It could be the whole seventieth week of Daniel, the great tribulation (usually attributed to the last three and a half years of Daniel's seventieth week), the day of the Lord, or something else altogether.

Summary

There are no scriptures pointing to the rapture being an imminent event. The rapture takes place at the beginning of the day of the Lord. The day of the Lord follows three events (cosmic disturbance, apostasy, the revealing of the man of lawlessness), and may also follow the coming of an Elijah. The rapture is not an imminent event.

Section 3

Conclusion

The conclusion to the matter

CHAPTER 14

The Semitic Style of Revelation

The seventh seal does not necessarily introduced the seven trumpets

And

The seventh trumpet does not necessarily introduce the seven bowls of wrath

The most popular theory of the order of events in the book of Revelation is as follows:

1st Seal
2nd Seal
3rd Seal
4th Seal
5th Seal
6th Seal
7th Seal–This seal according to this theory introduces the seven trumpets
   1st Trumpet
   2nd Trumpet
   3rd Trumpet
   4th Trumpet
   5th Trumpet
   6th Trumpet

7th Trumpet-This seal according to this theory introduces the seven bowls of wrath

1st Bowl
2nd Bowl
3rd Bowl
4th Bowl
5th Bowl
6th Bowl
7th Bowl

This theory is an assumption. Just as any idea on the order of the seals, trumpets, and bowls is a theory.

Given is the seventh seal found in Revelation 8:1, "When he opened the seventh seal, there was silence in heaven for about half an hour."

The Bible does not say the seventh seal contains the seven trumpets and seven bowls of wrath. This verse simply states, that there was silence in heaven for about half an hour.

Revelation 5:1-5, "Then I saw in the right hand of him who sat on the throne a scroll with writing on both sides and sealed with seven seals. And I saw a mighty angel proclaiming in a loud voice, "Who is worthy to break the seals and open the scroll?" But no one in heaven or on earth or under the earth could open the scroll or even look inside it. I wept and wept because no one was found who was worthy to open the scroll or look inside. Then one of the elders said to me, "Do not weep! See, the Lion of the tribe of Judah, the Root of David, has triumphed. He is able to open the scroll and its seven seals."

Some people believe the seven seal scroll contains the trumpets and bowls, but that is just an assumption. Neither the scroll in Rev 5:1-5 or the seventh seal of Rev 8:1 is said to contain the trumpets or bowls.

The seventh seal follows the cosmic disturbance of the sixth seal, the sealing of the 144,000 Jews, and the rapture of the church.

The silence in heaven for about half an hour *could* correspond to Zephaniah 1:7, "Be silent before the Sovereign LORD, for the day of the LORD is near. The LORD has prepared a sacrifice; he has consecrated those he has invited."

Or the silence in heaven for about half an hour *could* correspond to heaven being empty. The day of the Lord has begun. The angels have gathered the elect from the four winds after the shout of the archangel. Then the Lord will establish the millennial kingdom.

The silence in heaven is left to speculation at this point in history.

What is important to note is that the seventh seal is an individual seal with its own contents. Seals one through six each contain an event to transpire. The seventh seal also contains an event to transpire. As does each trumpet and bowl. Each trumpet has a specific event, and so does each bowl.

Likewise the seventh trumpet found in Revelation 11:15-19 does not contain the seven bowls. (The seventh angel sounded his trumpet, and there were loud voices in heaven, which said: "The kingdom of the world has become the kingdom of our Lord and of his Christ, and he will reign for ever and ever." And the twenty-four elders, who were seated on their thrones before God, fell on their faces and worshiped God, saying: "We give thanks to you, Lord God Almighty, the One who is and who was, because you have taken your great power and have begun to reign. The nations were angry; and your wrath has come. The time has come for judging the dead, and for rewarding your servants the prophets and your saints and those who reverence your name, both small and great—and for destroying those who destroy the earth." Then God's temple in heaven was opened, and within his temple was seen the ark of his covenant. And there came flashes of lightning, rumblings, peals of thunder, an earthquake and a great hailstorm.)

There is no indication in these verses of the seventh trumpet introducing the seven bowls. The Bible states the world has become the kingdom of our Lord and his Christ. Their reign will last forever. The seventh trumpet is the third woe.

The first woe is the fifth trumpet. The second woe is the sixth trumpet. The second woe is completed after the two witnesses go up to heaven in a cloud. (Rev 11:14)

The sixth seal, the seventh trumpet, and the seventh bowl converge at about the same time. At the end of Daniel's seventieth week

Sixth seal Revelation 6:12-17-

I watched as he opened the sixth seal. There was a great earthquake. The sun turned black like sackcloth made of goat hair, the whole moon turned blood red, and the stars in the sky fell to earth, as late figs drop from a fig tree when shaken by a strong wind. The sky receded like a scroll, rolling up, and every mountain and island was removed from its place. Then the kings of the earth, the princes, the generals, the rich, the mighty, and every slave and every free man hid in caves and among the rocks of the mountains. They called to the mountains and the rocks, "Fall on us and hide us from the face of him who sits on the throne and from the wrath of the Lamb! For the great day of their wrath has come, and who can stand?"

Seventh trumpet Revelation 11:15-19–

The seventh angel sounded his trumpet, and there were loud voices in heaven, which said: "The kingdom of the world has become the kingdom of our Lord and of his Christ, and he will reign for ever and ever." And the twenty-four elders, who were seated on their thrones before God, fell on their faces and worshiped God, saying: "We give thanks to you, Lord God Almighty, the One who is and who was, because you have taken your great power and have begun to reign. The nations were angry; and your wrath has come. The time has come for judging the dead, and for rewarding your servants the prophets and your saints and those who reverence your name, both small and great—and for destroying those who destroy the earth." Then God's temple in heaven was opened, and within his temple was seen the ark of his covenant. And there came flashes of lightning, rumblings, peals of thunder, an earthquake and a great hailstorm.

Seventh bowl Revelation 16:17-21

The seventh angel poured out his bowl into the air, and out of the temple came a loud voice from the throne, saying, "It is done!" Then there came flashes of lightning, rumblings, peals of thunder and a severe earthquake. No earthquake like it has ever occurred since man has been on earth, so tremendous was the quake. The great city split into three parts, and the cities of the nations collapsed. God remembered Babylon the Great and gave her the cup filled with the wine of the fury of his wrath. Every island fled away and the mountains could not be found. From the sky huge hailstones of about a hundred pounds each fell upon men. And they cursed God on account of the plague of hail, because the plague was so terrible.

The seven seals take us to the end of the seventieth week of Daniel.

1st seal is the rise of the Antichrist.

2nd seal is war.

3rd seal is economic chaos.

4th seal is death. One fourth of the world will perish due
    to sword, famine, plague, and by wild beasts.

5th seal is martyrdom.

6th seal is the cosmic disturbance. The cosmic disturbance
    occurs before the day of the Lord.

7th seal silence in heaven for about half an hour.

One could find a similarity of the order of the seals in the Olivet Discourse found in Matthew chapter 24. The sixth seal corresponds to Matthew 24:29.

1st	2nd	3rd	4th	5th	6th	7th
Seal	Seal	Seal	Seal	Seal	Seal	Seal

The order of the seals does go one through seven. The order of the trumpets and bowls both go one through seven. But the first trumpet does not follow the seventh seal, nor does the first bowl follow the seventh trumpet. The proof is given in the seals, trumpets, and bowls passages.

Given is the sounding of the fourth trumpet in Revelation 8:12, "The fourth angel sounded his trumpet, and a third of the sun was struck, a third of the moon, and a third of the stars, so that a third of them turned dark. A third of the day was without light, and also a third of the night."

The fourth trumpet must occur before the sixth seal. In the fourth trumpet a third of the sun, moon, and stars are darkened, but the sixth seal will have the darkened sun, the red blood moon, and the stars falling to the sky. (This is overlooked in the pre-tribulation rapture position. They ignore the Joel 2:30-31 and Acts 2:20 cosmic disturbance before the day of the Lord. They state the cosmic disturbance of the sixth seal is before the fourth trumpet, and at the end of the tribulation period the cosmic disturbance happens again in Matthew 24:29)

No one can state with any certainty when or how long each seal, trumpet, and bowl begins or ends.

All one can state is the fourth trumpet must occur before the sixth seal.

1st Seal	2nd Seal	3rd Seal	4th Seal			5th Seal		6th Seal		7th Seal
Trumpets			1st	2nd	3rd	4th	5th	6th		7th

We find the same scenario with the bowls relationship to the trumpets.

Given is second and third bowls in Revelation 16:3-7, "The second angel poured out his bowl on the sea, and it turned into blood like that of a dead man, and every living thing in the sea died.

The third angel poured out his bowl on the rivers and springs of water, and they became blood. Then I heard the angel in charge of the waters say: "You are just in these judgments, you who are and who were, the Holy One, because you have so judged; for they have shed the blood of your saints and prophets, and you have given them blood to drink as they deserve." And I heard the altar respond: "Yes, Lord God Almighty, true and just are your judgments."

The second trumpet had one third of the sea creatures die. The second bowl has every living thing in the sea die.

The third trumpet had one third of the springs become bitter. The third bowl has the springs become like blood.

1s Seal	2nd Seal	3rd Seal	4th Seal		5th Seal		6th Seal		7th Seal
Trumpets		1st	2nd	3rd	4th	5th	6th		7th
Bowls			1st	2nd	3rd	4th	5th	6th	7th

So, despite what one believes, the truth is the seventh seal does not contain seven angels with seven trumpets and seven angels who came out of the temple with seven bowls. Each individual seal, trumpet, and bowl is an individual event. The seventh seal does not produce seven angels with seven trumpets. The seventh trumpet does not produce seven angels with seven bowls.

The rapture takes place between the sixth and seventh seal.

After this I looked and there before me was a great multitude that no one could count, from every nation, tribe, people and language, standing before the throne and in front of the Lamb. They were wearing white robes and were holding palm branches in their hands. And they cried out in a loud voice:
"Salvation belongs to our God,
who sits on the throne,
and to the Lamb."
All the angels were standing around the throne and around the elders and the four living creatures. They fell down on their faces before the throne and worshiped God, saying:
"Amen!
Praise and glory
and wisdom and thanks and honor
and power and strength
be to our God for ever and ever. Amen!"
Then one of the elders asked me, "These in white robes—who are they, and where did they come from?"
I answered, "Sir, you know."
And he said, "These are they who have come out of the great tribulation; they have washed their robes and made them white in the blood of the Lamb. Therefore,

"they are before the throne of God
and serve him day and night in his temple;
and he who sits on the throne will spread his tent over them.
Never again will they hunger;
never again will they thirst.
The sun will not beat upon them,

nor any scorching heat.
For the Lamb at the center of the throne will be their shepherd;
he will lead them to springs of living water.
And God will wipe away every tear from their eyes." (Revelation 6:9-17)

The rapture takes place between the sixth and seven bowls

"Behold, I come like a thief! Blessed is he who stays awake and keeps his clothes with him, so that he may not go naked and be shamefully exposed." (Revelation 16:15)

It has already been discussed. The coming of the thief is a reference to the rapture. The unsaved will be surprised at the coming of our Lord Jesus Christ. The unsaved will be taken by surprised like a thief in the night.

The saved shall not be surprised at the coming of our Lord and Savior. They will have been the generation who saw all the signs proceeding the day of the Lord. They will be waiting for the revealing of our Lord Jesus Christ.

The rewarding of the saints takes place after the sounding of the seventh trumpet.

The seventh angel sounded his trumpet, and there were loud voices in heaven, which said:

"The kingdom of the world has become the kingdom of our Lord and of his Christ, and he will reign for ever and ever." And the twenty-four elders, who were seated on their thrones before God, fell on their faces and worshiped God, saying: "We give thanks to you, Lord God Almighty, the One who is and who was, because you have taken your great power and have begun to reign. The nations were angry; and your wrath has come. The time has come for judging the dead, and for rewarding your servants the prophets and your saints and those who reverence your name, both small and great—and for destroying those who destroy the earth." (Revelation 11:15-18)

This verse is damaging the pre-tribulation rapture position. The twenty-four elders are saying the time for rewarding of the saints has come. This contradicts their position. See box below.

The rewarding of the saints occurs at the end of the seventieth week of Daniel. Jesus sits on his throne with all the angels around him after the seventieth week of Daniel. Their on his throne will he judge. The rewarding of the saints occurs when the kingdom of this world has become the kingdom of our Lord and his Christ.

The Pre-tribulation Rapture Position of the Judgment Seat of Christ

The judgment seat of Christ is the rewarding of believers, not for the judgment of one's eternal state. The order of events follows:

1. The Rapture takes place
2. The judgment seat of Christ takes place between the rapture and the start of the seventieth week of Daniel. This would explain why there are 24 elders in front of the throne of God. In their opinion, this is proof of the rewarding of the raptured saints.
3. Some hold that the judgment seat of Christ starts at the rapture and continues throughout the seventieth week of Daniel.
4. This rewarding of saints at the seventh trumpet is to be the rewarding of tribulation saints and Old Testament saints. (In this position only New Testament saints take part in the rapture event)
5. The seventh trumpet unleashes the seven bowls of wrath.
6. Their fulfillment of the rewarding found in the seventh trumpet would take place in part 2b of the second coming of Jesus.

Revelation and Daniel are similar in structure

Daniel chapter two

The book of Daniel with its prophetic view of history is similar in style to the book of Revelation's overlapping seals, trumpets, and bowls. Daniel's prophecies are drawn out over a greater length of time. In Daniel, the prophecies begin with the first world empire, Babylon, and continue to the Ancient of Days pronounces judgment in favor of the saints of the Most High. In chapters 7, 8 and 11 more details are given concerning the same timeline.

Daniel's first look into the future involved King Nebuchadnezzar. King Nebuchadnezzar wanted to be told what his dream was, and what the meaning of the dream was. No one in his kingdom could do this, so King Nebuchadnezzar ordered the execution of all the wise men of Babylon. Daniel petitioned Arioch, the commander of the king's guard, for more time, so that he might interpret the dream.

Then Hananiah, Mishael, Azariah, and Daniel prayed. The dream and the meaning of the dream were revealed to Daniel.

"You looked, O king, and there before you stood a large statue—an enormous, dazzling statue, awesome in appearance. The head of the statue was made of pure gold, its chest and arms of silver, its belly and thighs of bronze, its legs of iron, its feet partly of iron and partly of baked clay. While you were watching, a rock was cut out, but not by human hands. It struck the statue on its feet of iron and clay and smashed them. Then the iron, the clay, the bronze, the silver and the gold were broken to pieces at the same time and became like chaff on a threshing floor in the summer. The wind swept them away without leaving a trace. But the rock that struck the statue became a huge mountain and filled the whole earth."

"This was the dream, and now we will interpret it to the king. You, O king, are the king of kings. The God of heaven has given you dominion and power and might and glory; in your hands he has placed mankind and the beasts of the field and the birds of the air. Wherever they live, he has made you ruler over them all. You are that head of gold."

"After you, another kingdom will rise, inferior to yours. Next, a third kingdom, one of bronze, will rule over the whole earth."

"Finally, there will be a fourth kingdom, strong as iron—for iron breaks and smashes everything—and as iron breaks things to pieces, so it will crush and break all the others. Just as you saw that the feet and toes were partly of baked clay and partly of iron, so this will be a divided kingdom; yet it will have some of the strength of iron in it, even as you saw iron mixed with clay. As the toes were partly iron and partly clay, so this kingdom will be partly strong and partly brittle. And just as you saw the iron mixed with baked clay, so the people will be a mixture and will not remain united, any more than iron mixes with clay."

"In the time of those kings, the God of heaven will set up a kingdom that will never be destroyed, nor will it be left to another people. It will crush all those kingdoms and bring them to an end, but it will itself endure forever. This is the meaning of the vision of the rock cut out of a mountain, but not by human hands—a rock that broke the iron, the bronze, the clay, the silver and the gold to pieces."

"The great God has shown the king what will take place in the future. The dream is true and the interpretation is trustworthy."

Head of Gold—Nebuchadnezzar-Babylon

Chest & Arms of Silver—Medo-Persian Empire

Belly & Thighs of Bronze—Greece

Legs of Iron—Rome

Feet & Ten Toes of Iron & Clay-Kingdom to come

The Rock-Jesus

The Rock (Jesus) will destroy the kingdoms. Jesus will establish his own kingdom that will never be destroyed.

This is Daniel's view of the kingdoms of the world down through the history of time. The time of the Gentiles shall end with the return of Jesus who will set up his kingdom on Earth.

We have Babylon, Medo-Persia, Greece, Rome, and some sort of confederacy of ten parts (ten toes) at the end of days. It is significant to note that in verse thirty-four, the rock (Jesus) strikes the last kingdom (the feet of iron and clay) and destroys all signs of the previous kingdoms.

Daniel chapter seven

Daniel sees four beasts come up out of the sea. (Rev 13:1 also sees the beast coming out of the sea) The four beasts are:

1st beast—It was like a lion and had four wings upon his back. Its wings were torn off its back, and it was lifted from the ground. It was stood on two feet like a man, and was given a heart of a man. This lion corresponds to the head of gold. It is Babylon.

2nd beast—It was like a bear. It was raised up on its side, and it had three ribs in its mouth between its teeth. It was told, "Get up and eat your fill of flesh!" This bear corresponds to the chest and arms of silver. It is the Medo-Persian Empire.

3rd beast—It was like a leopard, and on its back it had four wings like those of a bird. This beast had four heads, and it was given authority to rule. The four heads is very indicative of the split of the Grecian Empire after the death of Alexander the Great. The leopard corresponds to the belly and thighs of bronze. It is Greece.

4th beast—This beast was terrifying, frightening, and very powerful. It had large iron teeth. It crushed and devoured his victims and trampled underfoot whatever was left. It was different from all the rest. It had ten horns. This corresponds to the legs of iron. It is Rome.

While Daniel was thinking about the horns, another horn, a little one, came up among the ten horns. Three of the horns were uprooted. This horn had eyes like the eyes of a man and a mouth that spoke boastfully. Daniel is given the explanation of the little horn in verses 23-28.

The fourth beast will be a fourth kingdom that will appear on the earth. This kingdom will be different from all the other kingdoms. This kingdom will devour the whole earth, trampling it down and crushing it.

The ten horns are ten kings who will come from this kingdom. After them another king (the little horn) will arise, different from the earlier ones. This king will subdue three kings. This king will speak against the Most High. This king will wage war against the saints and will be defeating the saints. Then the Most High will pronounce judgment in favor of the saints, and the king (the little horn) will have his power taken away and will be completely destroyed.

The little horn is the Antichrist.

Near the end of the time of the Gentiles there will be an alliance of ten powers. Out of this alliance of ten powers, the Antichrist will emerge. Three of the ten powers will be subdued somehow by the Antichrist.

The ten horns correspond to the ten toes of iron and clay. This is a future alliance of ten powers. Some authors suggest a revival of the Roman Empire. Out of these ten horns comes the little horn, the Antichrist. The Antichrist will oppress the saints for three and a half years. Then Jesus, the rock, shall destroy him with the brightness of his coming.

Head of gold = beast like a lion = Babylon, Nebuchadnezzar

Chest and arms of silver = beast like a bear = Medo-Persia, Darius

Belly and thighs of bronze = beast like a leopard = Greece, Alexander the Great

Legs of iron = terrifying beast = Rome

Feet and ten toes of iron and clay = future ten power alliance-out of this ten power alliance, the little horn (Antichrist will arise)

Daniel chapter eight

In this vision Daniel sees a ram with two horns. Then a goat with a prominent horn between his eyes came from the west. The goat attacked the ram furiously and shattered both of its horns. The goat became very great, but at the height of his power, the large horn on the goat was broken off. In place of the horn, four prominent horns grew up.

We are told in verse twenty that the two-horned ram are the kings of Media and Persia.

In verse twenty-one, we are told that the goat is Greece, and the large horn is the first king who we now know was Alexander the Great. The four horns that replaced the one that was broken off represent four kingdoms that will emerge from his nation but will not have the same power. Alexander's empire was divided between four areas.

Out of the four horns, a little horn grew. This little horn is Antiochus Epiphanes, and he committed the abomination of desolation. He is a picture of the coming of the Antichrist.

Head of gold = beast like a lion = Babylon, Nebuchadnezzar

Chest and arms of silver = beast like a bear = Medo-Persia, Darius

Belly and thighs of bronze = beast like a leopard = goat with a large horn = Greece, Alexander the Great

Legs of iron = terrifying beast = Rome

Feet and ten toes of iron and clay = future ten power alliance-out of this ten power alliance, the little horn (Antichrist will arise)

Daniel chapter eleven goes on to tell more about the Medo-Persian Empire. There were four more kings to come. Then Alexander the Great conquered them. Then Alexander's empire was divided out toward the four winds of heaven. In this chapter, many battles and alliances are mentioned, and all of them have been fulfilled. Also mention is Antiochus Epiphanes and the willful king (Antichrist).

Summary

Daniel begins with the statue which is a look through history. The other chapters build upon the foundation of the statue. The other chapters give more details about certain kings, kingdoms, and events.

The same is true of the book of Revelation. The first seven seals take us through to the end of the times of the Gentiles. The trumpets and the bowls take place during the seven seals.

CHAPTER 15

Only Two Resurrections, Not Three

The erroneous assumption of a rapture before the seventieth week of Daniel has forced the pre-tribulation rapture position to believe in three resurrections of the dead instead of only two resurrections.

The pre-tribulation rapture position believes the rapture and the resurrection of the New Testament saints occur before the seventieth week of Daniel. They believe the resurrection at the rapture only includes the New Testament saints, the ones who believe in Jesus. They quote 1 Thessalonians 4:16 as their proof of the resurrection at the rapture as a Christian only experience at that time.

It is never mentioned in the Bible that only the New Testament saints would be resurrected at the rapture. This is only an assumption based on the fact that Paul did not mention the Old Testament saints. Just because something is not mentioned does not mean it is excluded by omission. The word church is not mention in eternity or the millennium. Nor is the word Bible mentioned in the Bible.

In Daniel chapter 12, Daniel only tells of two resurrections. One resurrection is to everlasting life, and the other resurrection is to everlasting contempt.

> But at that time your people—everyone whose name is found written in the book—will be delivered. Multitudes who sleep in the dust of the earth will awake: some to everlasting life, others to shame and everlasting contempt. Daniel 12:1-2

We find only two resurrections in Revelation. In Revelation chapter twenty, we find that those who are part of the first resurrection are blessed and the second death shall have no power over them. We also find here in Revelation twenty that there is a period of at least one thousand years between the first and second resurrections.

The pre-tribulation rapture position takes the rising the martyrs mentioned in Rev 20:4 and links the martyrs resurrection with resurrection of the Old Testament saints (those holy people who died before Jesus died)

For the pre-tribulation rapture position to be accurate with the Bible, the Bible must call the resurrection of the martyrs and the Old Testament saints the second resurrection. But this is not the case. The Bible calls the resurrection of the martyrs as the first resurrection.

So again, for the pre-tribulation rapture position there are three resurrections to their theory. They are given below.

1. Resurrected New Testament saints at the pre-tribulation rapture before the seventieth week of Daniel
2. Resurrection of the martyrs of the tribulation period and Old Testament saints at the end of the seventieth week of Daniel.
3. Resurrection of the wicked to be judged at the Great White Throne Judgment one thousand plus years at the conclusion of the seventy weeks of Daniel.

But there are only two resurrections listed in the Bible. One Resurrection is to everlasting life, and one resurrection is to everlasting contempt.

Following the cosmic disturbance, the Lord Jesus shall descend from heaven. The dead in Christ, both the Old and New Testament saints, shall have their dead bodies raised from the grave. The dead bodies shall be change from the mortal, corruptible body to a glorified, immortal, incorruptible body. They shall meet the Lord in the air. (the rapture)

Those who are alive at the second coming of Jesus shall also have their mortal bodies changed into immortal bodies. They shall also meet the Lord in the air. (the rapture)

The saints along with the angels now accompany Jesus all the way down to the earth. (The Bible never states that Jesus comes from Heaven to the clouds of the earth, and then seven plus years later he comes back from Heaven for a third time all the way to the earth. It is one second coming of Jesus.)

Jesus destroys the assembled armies at the battle of Armageddon.

Jesus will sit in Jerusalem.

He will judge the survivors of the nations. Those who have helped Jesus' brothers and have not taken the mark of the beast shall enter the millennial kingdom. Those who did not help Jesus' brothers will be sent away to everlasting punishment.

Satan will be locked in the Abyss for a thousand years.

After the one thousand years are over, Satan will be let loose to deceive the nations. How long Satan is let loose, is never mentioned. But God will put an end to this last rebellion.

The wicked shall now be raised from the dead. This is the second resurrection. The wicked dead will be judged at the Great White Throne Judgment. The wicked dead after their hearing shall be cast into the lake of burning fire.

Then there will be a new heavens and a new earth. Then the Holy City, Jerusalem, shall descend out of Heaven. God has prepared it as bride beautifully dressed for her husband Eternity. God with man, Heaven on Earth.

CHAPTER 16

Conclusion

When the Son of Man comes, will he find faith on the earth?" (Luke 18:8) This is an excellent question.

Apostasy will reign in the end of days. They will believe the lie. The Christian will have to make a decision during the reign of the Antichrist. Will the Christian choose Jesus? Or will the Christian succumb to the pressure of the times and take the mark of the beast?

Most will choose this world and the things this world offers. Brother will betray brother, a father his son, and a daughter her mother. Although some might feign allegiance to the Antichrist for the sake of buying and selling in the future economy of the beast, their fate will be sealed at the willful taking of the mark of the beast. The lake of burning fire will be for those who receive the mark of the beast.

The children of the light will be exposed. The Christian will not be able to trade or be legally employed unless the Christian swears his allegiance to the man of lawlessness who will sit in the temple in Jerusalem.

The true Christians will be hunted down. Satan knows his time is short. Satan through the Antichrist will imprison and kill those holding to the testimony of Jesus. The saints will be handed over to the Antichrist for three and a half years. (You might think this scenario is impossible because you will be raptured before you have to endure persecution. Think again. Just ignore the persecutions the early church suffered, and just look at the last one hundred years. Hitler, Stalin, and China are just some examples. Those three have killed millions of Christians.)

The sun will turn black and the moon to blood red after the distress of those days.

Then the Ancient of days shall step in. Jesus and the angels shall come from heaven to the clouds of the earth. The earth will see the return of Jesus.

With a loud shout and the command of the archangel, the dead will rise (those saints from both the Old and the New Testament). This is the first resurrection. Blessed is he who takes part in the first resurrection. The second death will have no hold on him.

Those who are of the faith and still alive at the second coming of Jesus will have their mortal body changed to an immortal body. For when Jesus appears, he shall transform his brothers' lowly bodies to the likeness of Jesus, himself. Then they shall be caught up in the clouds with Jesus, the angels, and the resurrected dead.

144,000 Jews will be sealed. This sealing will protect them from the dreadful part of the day of the Lord. Whether or not this is a visible mark is uncertain. This sealing of the Holy Spirit is not a visible mark, but the blood over the door post during the Passover was clearly seen.

Jesus will lead the armies of heaven on a white horse down to the assembled armies of Armageddon. His feet shall land on the Mount of Olives. He shall destroy the enemies of God. The blood will flow for over 180 miles, but Jerusalem will be saved out of it.

Jesus will capture the beast and the false prophet. Jesus will throw the beast and the false prophet into the lake of burning fire. Satan shall be caught. Satan will be thrown into the abyss for a thousand years.

Jesus will establish his kingdom on earth.

Though man will be scarcer than pure gold, some will still be left alive. Those survivors will go through the judgment of the Gentiles or nations. The survivors will face Jesus. Those who have not received the mark of the beast and have helped Jesus' brothers (Christians and Jews) in need will enter the millennial kingdom. Those who have not helped Jesus' brothers will be sent to everlasting punishment.

It is as simple as that. There is not part 2a and 2b to the second coming of Jesus. There is not a coming in the clouds of Christ to receive their resurrected immortal bodies and to catch up those saints who are alive and then return to heaven to live in the New Jerusalem for seven years. Then seven plus years come back to earth with Jesus. Have another resurrection this time with Old Testament saints and the tribulation saints, and then live in the millennial kingdom.

It is one coming of the King of Kings. He shall call all of the saints out of the grave, transform all the bodies of those still alive, and catch up the believers in the clouds. Then the dreadful part of the day of the Lord begins on the unbelieving.

Marvin Rosenthal said it best, "To tell the church that it will not be present during a significant part of the seventieth week of Daniel is to court disaster. Such an attitude will result in a church totally unprepared for the conflict, laboring under the misconception that they will not be present.[37]

The church needs to be told the truth, not the fantasy. It took one madman, Hitler, to bring about the death of 6,000,000 Jews in less than ten years. And Hitler was not even the Antichrist. Things can turn in this country and across the world in no time. The church must be prepared for tribulation and the great tribulation to come.

---

[37] Marvin Rosenthal, The Pre-wrath Rapture of the Church(Tennessee: Thomas Nelson, Inc, 1990), 138

CHAPTER 17

Questions and Answers

Is not the church and Israel to be on separate programs?

This is held firmly by the pre-tribulation rapture position. They hold to an interpretation of the Bible known as Dispensationalism.

Dispensationalism is a manmade commentary and/or interpretation on the Bible. It has been given importance by man.

Dispensationalism superimposed on the Bible can be compared to the Mishna, Gemara, Midrashim, and Kabbala. These books were superimposed upon the law. This superimposition transferred obedience from the law itself to the traditional interpretations.[38] The Pharisees and the Sadducees of Jesus' day were guilty of this.

The most common seven dispensations are given:

1. Innocence–Genesis 1:28
2. Conscience–Genesis 3:7
3. Human Government–Genesis 8:15
4. Promise–Genesis 12:1
5. The Law-Exodus 19:1
6. Church–Acts 2:1
7. Kingdom

---

[38]   Oxford NIV Scofield Study Bible(1984 edition),964

Some use Dispensationalism to prove a pre-tribulation rapture position. They claim the seven economies are successive. The pattern goes 1,2,3,4,5, and 6, but then the rapture occurs before the beginning of Daniel's seventieth week. It is believed that the end of the church era is the evacuation of the church by a pre-tribulation rapture.[39] Then God reverts back to the law dispensation (No.5). But this second phase of the law economy will only last seven plus years, and then it will end with the seventh economy, the Kingdom. Their pattern would go like 1,2,3,4,5,6,5, and then 7.

A question needs to be asked. Why would there be a progressive formula up to the beginning of Daniel's seventieth week and then a regression?

The answer is since Dispensationalism is a manmade supposition, man can change his theory to fit his own conclusions. We see this in scientific observations. Theories are put forth as truths to support a political or social position agenda. Data manipulated to draw a certain conclusion.

The Times of the Gentiles began with the captivity of Judah under Nebuchadnezzar of the Babylonians. The Times of the Gentiles continues through the seventieth week of Daniel. Both Jew and Gentile were present for the first sixty-nine weeks. Both Jew and Gentile will be present during the final week of Daniel's prophecy.

The Law Dispensation (No.5) began after the Exodus. The Church Dispensation (no.6) began at the day of Pentecost at the outpouring of the Holy Spirit. Remember the pre-tribulation rapture position believes the Holy Spirit will be removed because the Holy Spirit indwells each believer. They believe the Holy Spirit through the Church must be removed before the man of lawlessness is revealed. They overlook the Acts and Joel passages which have the outpouring of the Holy Spirit to the cosmic disturbance.

Daniel's seventy weeks began around 445 B.C. with the decree to rebuild the wall by Artaxerxes. The Times of the Gentiles began at least 141 years earlier.

Dispensationalists use the seventy weeks of Daniel to state that God is dealing with the nation of Israel during the last week. The time between the sixty-ninth and the seventieth week is the church age. The seventieth week of Daniel they believe is the resumption of God dealing with Israel again, not the church.

---

39   Hal Lindsey, The Rapture(New York: Bantam Books,1983),74

But during both the Law Dispensation and the Church dispensation, Jerusalem will be trampled on by the Gentiles. Even though Israel now controls all of Jerusalem, Jerusalem is still trampled on by the Gentiles. The Dome of the Rock may be sitting upon the temple mount. The Times of the Gentiles shall end after the last forty-two months of Daniel's seventieth week (Rev 11). At the end of the Times of the Gentiles, Jesus shall establish his kingdom on earth.

The theory of Dispensationalism would work just fine with the post-tribulation rapture position. It would take the church economy from the day of Pentecost to the cosmic disturbance without any regressions of their economies. In the post-tribulation rapture position, the Kingdom Dispensation would naturally follow the Church Dispensation. And, any person who comes to a knowledge and acceptance of Jesus as their Savior during the seventieth week of Daniel would be part of the church, the bride of Christ.

Even though Israel and the Church are to be grafted together into the vine, Israel does have a destiny distinct from the Church. The Abrahamic and Davidic covenants are to be fulfilled. Israel will be the capital of the earth with Jesus ruling from Jerusalem. Each year people from around the globe will go up to Israel to worship. The Millennial Kingdom is the promised kingdom whose David's seed will rule forever. As the church, we will be co-heirs with Jesus of the promised kingdom.

The Church has never replaced Israel, and Israel will not replace the Church. We eventually will be one in Christ.

Why did you not mention Dispensationalism in this book?

Since Dispensationalism is a manmade interpretation of the Bible, I will give it no credence.

Is the rapture part of the day of the Lord?

The day of the Lord is great, glorious, and dreadful. I agree with Marvin Rosenthal (pre-wrath rapture), John Walvoord (pre-tribulation rapture), and Robert Gundry (post-tribulation rapture) that the rapture is part or the start of the day of the Lord. The rapture would be part of the great and glorious part of the day of the Lord. The destruction of the armies and the valley of blood for 180 miles would be part of the dreadful day of the Lord.

If the revealing of the man of lawlessness is at the abomination of desolation, then why not the mid-tribulation rapture? The mid-tribulation rapture follows the abomination of desolation, and the day of the Lord beginning around the midpoint of the seventieth week of Daniel.

This is a very good point and question.

In the mid-tribulation position, the last seven bowls are the bowls of wrath. They are last because with them God's wrath is complete.

The seven bowls according to the mid-tribulation rapture position cover the last three and a half years of Daniel's seventieth week. Some pre-tribulation rapture believers hold to the same theory.[40]

For the seven bowls to cover three and a half years just does not seem reasonable. A lot of commentators put the seven bowls closely at the end of Daniel's seventieth week, or even after the cosmic disturbance. The reason for this is the severity of the bowl judgments. Man just cannot survive. For example:

1. *All* fresh water is turned to blood when the third bowl is poured out. Earlier with the third trumpet, one third of the water became undrinkable. If the seven bowls take place over a three and a half year period, the ruining of all fresh water would occur with one to three years remaining to Armageddon. Man and animal cannot live without water. Armies cannot move into position without proper logistics (water being a big issue).

2. The scorching sun of the fourth bowl makes it impossible for the seven bowls to be part of the day of the Lord. The day of the Lord follows the cosmic disturbance, and this unique day last through the dreadful part of the day of the Lord. The day of the Lord will have a dark sun and blood red moon. The mid-tribulation rapture believer cannot call the last three and a half years of Daniel's seventieth week part of the day of the Lord.

So, the apostasy and the man of lawlessness being revealed does give some weight to the mid-tribulation rapture position, and in their position

---

40   Tim LaHaye, The Rapture(Oregon: Harvest House Publishing,2002),64

they believe Elijah to be one of the two witnesses and their ministry taking place in the first half of Daniel's seventieth week. But, what is left out is the cosmic disturbance, and the cosmic disturbance must occur before the day of the Lord and the rapture.

Who will populate the Millennial Kingdom if the saints are raptured at the end of the seventieth week of Daniel?

This is the big question posed against the post-tribulation rapture stance. The answer is found in Matthew chapter twenty-five. There we find the judgment of the nations or otherwise known as the judgment of the sheep and goats. There will be people left on the earth after Armageddon. They will face Jesus in Jerusalem. Those people who have helped Jesus' brothers and have not received the mark of the beast will enter the Millennial Kingdom.

Who are the brothers of Jesus?

Jesus' brothers are those who do God's will. They listen and obey his voice.

These brothers are unique in the fact that these sheep (the followers of Jesus are called sheep and Jesus is the good shepherd) did not recognize the shepherd's (Jesus) voice. They are not Christians, but they helped the Christians and the Jews during the seventieth week of Daniel. They get to enter the Millennial Kingdom because of their obedience in helping the brethren. They did not recognize the voice of the shepherd. They even question Jesus as to when they helped his brothers out. These sheep will enter the Millennial Kingdom along with the Israelites who have survived. They will repopulate the earth.

The goats in this judgment did not respond to the voice. They did not help Jesus' brothers when they were in need. The goats are guilty, and they are sent away to everlasting punishment.

Is the rapture the blessed hope?

The Bible never calls the rapture the Blessed Hope. Our hope is in Jesus. Titus 2:13 is translated: looking for the blessed hope and appearing of the glory of the great God and our Saviour Jesus Christ (ASV)

Looking for that blessed hope, and the glorious appearing of the great God and our Saviour Jesus Christ (KJV) while we wait for the blessed hope—the glorious appearing of our great God and Savior, Jesus Christ (NIV)

If one wants to call the Blessed Hope the rapture, that is fine. There is just no Biblical basis for calling the rapture the Blessed Hope. It is just an assumption. Calling the rapture the Blessed Hope does not enhance or support any rapture position.

Does not the wrath of God begin with the opening of the first seal?

The Bible does not say this.

The great day of their (God and the Lamb) wrath does not begin until after opening of the sixth seal. Rev 6:17 states, "For the great day of their wrath has come, and who can stand?"

The "has come" draws controversy. It is from the Greek word, *erchomai.*

ERCHOMAI-come
1. To come a. of persons
1. to come from one place to another and used both of persons arriving
2. to appear, make one's appearance, come before public
2. Metaph.
a. to come into being, arise, come forth, show itself, find a place of influence b. to establish, be known, to come (fall) into or unto
3. To go, to follow one

The pre-tribulation rapture position, believes the wrath has come to be retroactive to the first seal. The other position does not hold that theory. The post-tribulation rapture position believes the wrath of the Lamb and God is about to begin at the sixth seal.

Two other scriptures with *erchomai* defined as "has come" or "is come" are given.

1. Mark 14:41—Returning the third time, he said to them, "Are you still sleeping and resting? Enough! The hour has come. Look, the Son of Man is delivered into the hands of sinners.

This verse just like Rev 6:17 has the *erchomai* about ready to happen. There is an event about ready to transpire.

2. Let us rejoice and be glad and give him glory! For the wedding of the Lamb has come, and his bride has made herself ready. (Rev 19:7)

Again this is an event to happen, not one that is occurring or started in the past.

The wrath of God is not limited to the day of the Lord. When discussing eschatology, it seems that every mention of the wrath of God belongs to the time of the end, but this is not the case.

In the New Testament the Greek word *orge* is translated into the word wrath. John 3:36 gives a good definition on what the wrath of God is. (Whoever believes in the Son has eternal life, but whoever rejects the Son will not see life, for God's wrath remains on them.) The wrath of God falls on the unbeliever. The sons of the light will not endure God's wrath. God's wrath is not the last week of Daniel. The day of the Lord is an outpouring of the wrath of God and the Lamb on the unrighteous.

But does not 1 Thessalonians 5:9 state, "For God did not appoint us to suffer wrath,"?

Yes, that is exactly what the verse states, but there are more words to this verse.

The pre-tribulation rapture position stops this quoting on 1 Thess 5:9 after the word wrath. His explanation is that the church will not endure the seventieth week of Daniel. He equates this last week of Daniel with the day of the Lord (a period of God's wrath). Therefore the Christian will be exempt from the seventieth week of Daniel because the whole seven years are this period of God's wrath.

This position ignores the rest of verse nine and the completion of Paul's sentence in verse ten. Given is 1 Thessalonians 5:9-10, "For God did not appoint us to suffer wrath but to receive salvation through our Lord Jesus Christ. He died for us so that, whether we are awake or asleep, we may live together with him."

Man was not meant to suffer the eternal fire. The eternal fire was prepared for the devil and his angels. God did not appoint us to suffer the wrath of God, but he sent his one and only Son that whoever believes in him shall not perish but have eternal life.

Jesus died for us. So if we die (asleep) we shall be with Jesus. While we are alive, we can walk the narrow road and be with Jesus. We will have tribulation in this world. We will have persecution. Persecution is to be expected for the believer. The world hates the Christian. The Christian will be saved from the day of the Lord (the wrath of God) by the rapture. The rapture will save the Christians who are still alive at the second coming of Jesus from the wrath of God.

What about Matthew 24:36? (No one knows about that day or hour, not even the angels in heaven, nor the Son, but only the Father.) Is this not a rapture passage? And does this not show imminence of the rapture?

This verse is sometimes used by those of the pre-tribulation rapture position as a rapture passage. Nobody on earth can tell you when the return of Jesus is going to take place.

In this verse, the day it is talking about is "that day."

"That day" is an antecedent. An antecedent means a preceding or prior circumstance, event, object, or style.

When Jesus was talking about "that day," he was probably referring back to the day the Son of Man would appear in the sky. (Matthew 24:30)

We will not know the exact day or hour of his return. (Such as-Jesus returns in 4 years, 6 days, 23 hours, and 43 seconds) But we do know that 3 events will happen before "that day."

1. Apostasy (Matthew 24:5,24
2. The revealing of the man of lawlessness at the abomination of desolation (Matthew 24:15)
3. The cosmic disturbance (Matthew 24:29)

We will not know the date, but we will know the signs that will come before "that day."

BIBLIOGRAPHY

Crowley, Dale. The Soon Coming of Our Lord. Washington, D.C.: The Capitol Voice Press, 1958

Gundry, Robert. The Church and the Tribulation. Michigan: The Zondervan Corporation, 1973

Hitchcock, Mark and Ice, Thomas. The Truth Behind Left Behind. Oregon: Multnomah Publishers, 2004

Lahaye, Tim. The Rapture. Oregon: Harvest House Publishers, 2002

Lindsey, Hal. The Rapture. New York: Bantam Books, 1983

Oxford NIV Scofield Study Bible. 1984 edition

Pentecost, J. Dwight. Prophecy for Today. Michigan: Discovery House Publishers, 1989

Rosenthal, Marvin. The Pre-wrath Rapture of the Church. Tennessee: Thomas Nelson Inc., 1990

Ryrie, Charles C. First and Second Thessalonians. Chicago: Moody Press, 2001

Strong's Number Reference from The word Bible Collection CD, 2006

Walvoord, John. The Rapture Question. Grand Rapids: Zondervan Publishing House, 1979

Made in the USA
Coppell, TX
18 April 2021